# Silver Dollar Tabor

# SILVER DOLLAR TABOR
## The Leaf in the Storm

By

Evelyn E. Livingston Furman

THE NATIONAL WRITERS PRESS
1982

FIRST EDITION

International Standard Book Number: 0-88100-013-2
Library of Congress Number: 82-82214

Printed in the United States of America by
The National Writers Press
1450 S. Havana
Aurora, Colorado 80012.

# Table of Contents

# Acknowledgments

My special thanks go to my daughter Sharon P. Furman Martin for typing the manuscript. I am also grateful to the following:

The Historical Society of Colorado

Denver Public Library, Western History Department

The Denver Post

The Leadville Herald Democrat

Colorado Magazine

Leadville City Directories

Other sources of material were from the author's collection of old newspaper clippings and stories from old time residents of Leadville who remembered many of the events mentioned.

The Tabor Collection, in the archives of the Historical Society of Colorado, contains many letters, photographs and other materials saved by Baby Doe Tabor. My special thanks go to the Society for the use of these items.

The subject of my story is Rosemary Echo Silver Dollar Tabor. The interesting and informative letters, many reproduced in her own handwriting, give the reader an accurate and inside look at her life. I have used many of her actual letters in an endeavor to clear up many misconceptions that have been written about the Tabor family in the past.

This book was written for the tourists and guests who have toured the Tabor Opera House in Leadville. After the tour many of the visitors stay to ask me more about Silver Dollar Tabor. In this book I have made every effort to include answers to the many questions usually asked.

Evelyn E. Livingston Furman
815 Harrison Avenue
Leadville, Colorado

# *Preface*

In this saga of the Tabors, the leading characters are now deceased. But the incredible story lives on.

Silver's life is inexorably interwoven with her other family members—thus my story includes those who were close to her. She was born into tremendous wealth, only to face complete poverty at an early age—along with the rest of her family.

In seeking success Silver should be given credit for her frequent and futile attempts. She experienced dozens of disappointments and failures throughout her young life. She became prey for numerous undesirable characters who tried, often with success, to take advantage of this frustrated and beautiful woman. When she needed guidance she steadfastly refused offers of help from her family.

She seemed to be destined to avoid all of the good things in life, following instead a rocky road that ultimately led to despair and destruction. Hers was the beginning of a beautiful life which became a wasted existence, a child traveling a road with no return, ending in a horrifying climax.

## Chapter One
# A Child Was Born

"Oh, her voice has the ring of a *silver dollar!*" Those were the words of William Jennings Bryan. The year was 1889, and he had come to Colorado, being greatly interested in the silver dispute of the time. Having heard so much of the wealthy Silver King of Colorado, H.A.W. Tabor, he called on the Tabors while in the state. The Tabors were living in a beautiful mansion located in Denver's finest residential section.

Mr. Bryan wanted to talk to Mr. Tabor about the future of silver and the Leadville mines.

At the time of his visit, the Tabors' second daughter (by his second wife) was only a few weeks old, having been born December 17, 1889. Her parents, Horace and Elizabeth Tabor, were anxious to show off their child to their distinguished guest. Mr. Bryan admired the little laughing beauty while her parents beamed with pleasure. Horace Tabor, hearing Mr. Bryan's words, *silver dollar*, was visibly impressed. The Tabors had not named the child as yet. Immediately Mr. Tabor exclaimed, "That's it, that's it—we will name her Silver Dollar!" Thus the famous William Jennings Bryan had named this Tabor baby. The names Rosemary and Echo were added. So the child had the name Rosemary Echo Silver Dollar Tabor, and was often fondly referred to as Honeymaid.

In a letter of January 13, 1890, Tilly Haben, Baby Doe's sister, writes from Oshkosh, Wisconsin, about the birth of her second daughter, Silver:

Silver had an older sister, the first child of the famous Tabors, Elizabeth Bonduel Lily, born July 13, 1884. She was a beautiful child and resembled her mother. Her disposition was very much like that of her father and other members of his family.

Baby Tabor was taken to Wisconsin to be christened at the age of three months. Mrs. Tabor was formerly from Oshkosh and her family still resided there. The christening outfit was "fit for a little princess," and cost fifteen thouand dollars!

The exquisite point duchess lace used to fashion this robe was delicately woven in a lily pattern. The white silk skirt with a tiny waist was one and half yards long and several yards around. Two deep flounces were draped over the skirt. A cascade of rare lace adorned the front of the dress. A brocaded velvet cape was of the same matching lily pattern. The cape and skirt were of the same length. This heavy satin-lined cape had two ruffles of matching lace which trimmed the entire edge. To complete this costly outfit, there was a tiny velvet cap banded with delicate ostrich feathers, and frilled with point duchess lace.

*Harper's Bazar* featured Baby Tabor in their winter holiday number when she was two and a half years old, a laughing,

Oakland Jan. 13/80.

Dear Lizzie,

We all send
you congratulations upon
your recovery, and the birth
of a little daughter, I did
not like to write you before,
as I was afraid you were not
as well as we would like,
Mother wrote me that you
had a dreadful time, I am so
sorry as the easiest time
is too hard, and then to have
more to go through is almost
more than one can stand,
but try and not think about
it, but that you have another
lovely daughter, and that you

will have the comfort of
seeing her grow up, and to
be a charming companion
to Cupid, I hope Mother &
Claudie will write often and
let us know how you are &
how keep thinking about you
most of the time.
Kindly remember us to [Mary?]
and kiss the little babies for
us, Andrew and all send
love and good wishes for the
coming year to all
                Affectionately
                Lily [Hepburn].

4

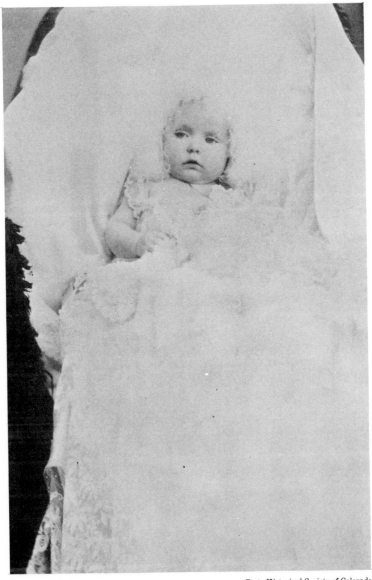

Lily (Baby) Tabor in her $15,000 christening gown that was "fit for a little princess."

Lily, "a winsome little girl with eyes as blue as forget-me-nots."

Lily was featured in the January 8, 1887 issue of *Harper's Bazar.* She was often photographed by leading Denver photographers.

Lily (Baby) Tabor at the age of 24 months.

Lily at 24 months in a lavish lace party dress.

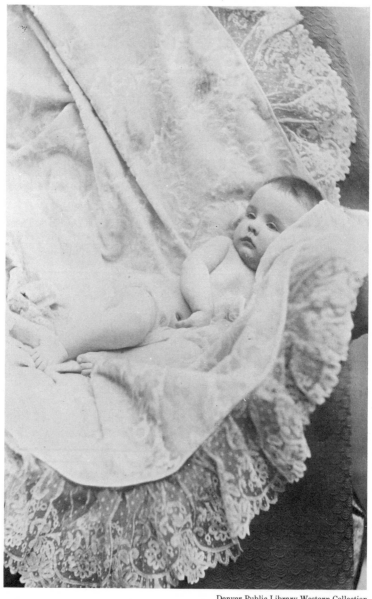

One of the first photographs of Rosemary Echo Silver Dollar Tabor.

**Silver Dollar in her christening gown. "Her voice has the ring of a silver dollar," said William Jennings Bryan.**

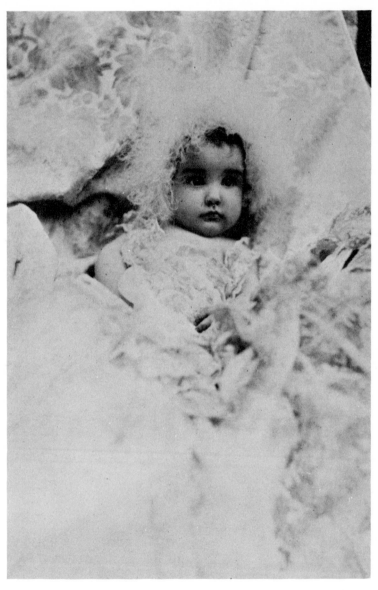

**Rosemary Echo Silver Dollar Tabor at the age of 16 weeks.**

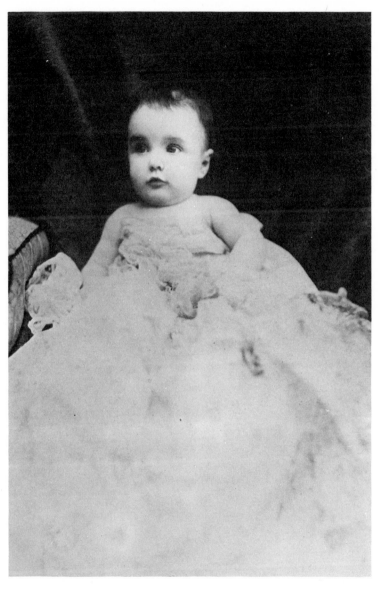

**Silver Dollar was as charming as her sister Lily—age 19 weeks.**

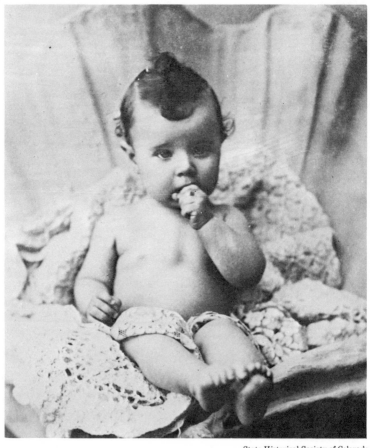

**Every pin used in the Tabor babies' clothes had a diamond at the top. Note the ring on Silver's finger.**

Silver Dollar poses in a pensive mood at the mansion's iron gate.

**Silver never lost her obsession for animals, from her days as a child until her last days in Chicago.**

Lily poses with a dove. Showing talent as an actress when young,
she never pursued acting as a career.

**Photographers were delighted when taking photographs of Lily for even as a child she posed herself.**

Lily was a happy little girl, laughing most of the time. An unusual pensive moment here.

A few of the expensive jewelry items and ornaments worn by
the Tabor daughters.

winsome little girl with eyes as blue as forget-me-nots. Her beautiful blonde hair was like spun gold. The artist, Thomas Nast, did the picture for January 8, 1887 *Harper's Bazar* which was an artistic frontispiece. Baby Tabor's picture was partly encircled with vines of ivy, juniper, and holly. She was one of the best known babies in the West, and was the idol of her father. Families of such wealth as the Tabors usually employed a nurse to care for their children, but her mother preferred to care for the child without the help of a nurse. Every pin used in Baby Tabor's clothes had a diamond at the top. There were gold clasps on her clothes, also set with diamonds. In spite of her costly wardrobe and myriads of small sparkling diamonds, Baby Tabor was not a spoiled child. She was a happy little tot, laughing most of the time. She very seldom cried.

Baby Tabor was often photographed by the leading Denver artists. She would pose herself perfectly without help from the photographer. The second child of Baby Doe and Horace Tabor had been a son, Horace Joseph, who died soon after birth (born October 17—died October 17, 1888).

Horace Austin Warner (H.A.W.) Tabor was born in Orleans County, Vermont, on November 26, 1830. His parents were not wealthy and he had few educational opportunities, gaining his knowledge, as they say, in the arena of life. A stone-cutter by trade, he was both active and ambitious. At about age 25 he was in Maine traveling by train with a friend when he met a stone contractor who was looking for help. He hired both Horace and his friend.

On this new job Tabor met Augusta Pierce, daughter of his employer. She was a beautiful young lady and they fell in love at first sight. When he asked for her hand in marriage she accepted and they became engaged. Horace began to look for greener pastures in preparation for his marriage and heeded the call of the West. He left the stone quarries of New England and homesteaded 160 acres in Riley County, Kansas. Two years later he returned to New England where he and Augusta were married in the Pierce home on January 31, 1857.

He took his bride back to the homestead in Kansas. Like all early day pioneers they experienced many hardships on the open prairie, but the Tabors met the challenge. Augusta worked in the fields after finishing her household tasks. But farming did not prove profitable, with drought one year and an abundant harvest the next resulting in an oversupply and no market for the crops. From the start, Horace was involved in politics in addition to farming, and was a member of the Kansas legislature when Kansas became a state.

Early in 1859 news of the Pike's Peak Gold Rush reached the ears of the Tabors who decided this was a good opportunity to make some money to pay for their 160 acres of government land, planning to look for gold in the summer and return to their homestake in the fall. Horace went to nearby Fort Riley and worked as a stone cutter to finance the trip.

Adding to the difficulties of the trip was their first-born child, Maxcy, born October 9, 1857, who had been sickly. Two men offered to accompany them to help along the way. The oxen pulled their covered wagon which was loaded with all their belongings and supplies. Again they were forced to endure the many hardships of the early day pioneers before finally arriving in Colorado, at a place now called Denver.

Horace followed the prospectors to Clear Creek, then on to Gregory diggings and Payne's Bar, now Idaho Springs. All summer he prospected for gold.

When winter arrived an old miner convinced Horace that he should get his wife and child out of the mountains because of the severe weather. He took the family back to Denver, but he returned to his prospect (claim). Here he found that the miner who had given him advice had jumped his prospect. Horace lost out on this occasion and all his summer work was for naught.

After spending the winter in Denver they started another long and difficult journey to California Gulch near the present site of Leadville, high in the Colorado Rockies. Abe Lee had made a rich discovery there and set off another rush.

Augusta Tabor was the first white woman to arrive in those parts. The miners all pitched in and built a cabin of green pine logs for the Tabors. Prospecting, combined with some mining

A log cabin constructed of black walnut logs was the first house the Tabor's built in Kansas, no longer in existence. This is the Tabor school, located near the Tabor homestead. It is located near Zeandale, Kansas, in an area now called the Tabor Valley.

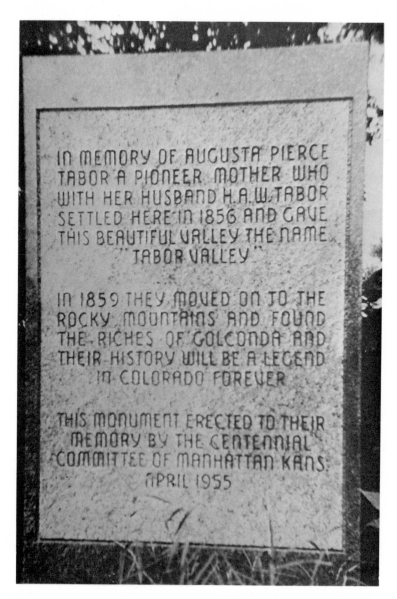

IN MEMORY OF AUGUSTA PIERCE
TABOR A PIONEER MOTHER WHO
WITH HER HUSBAND H.A.W. TABOR
SETTLED HERE IN 1856 AND GAVE
THIS BEAUTIFUL VALLEY THE NAME
"TABOR VALLEY"

IN 1859 THEY MOVED ON TO THE
ROCKY MOUNTAINS AND FOUND
THE RICHES OF GOLCONDA AND
THEIR HISTORY WILL BE A LEGEND
IN COLORADO FOREVER

THIS MONUMENT ERECTED TO THEIR
MEMORY BY THE CENTENNIAL
COMMITTEE OF MANHATTAN KANS.
APRIL 1955

The author visited Tabor Valley and photographed this monument in front of the Tabor schoolhouse near their stone house.

This is the Tabor homestead located near Zeandale, Kansas.

success, brought Horace $5,000 that season, and he decided to open up a general merchandise store in a new settlement named Oro. By the end of the next year Tabor had reaped $15,000 from his new enterprise.

When the gold excitement dwindled in this area and new discoveries were made over the mountain range, another booming mining camp called Buckskin Joe sprang up. The Tabors followed the miners and opened up an even larger store. H.A.W. Tabor rapidly became well known as a leading merchant and the town's postmaster.

## Chapter Two
# *The Horn of Plenty*

Oro again became active in mining, and then came the second great mining discovery—the Printer Boy Mine. The Tabors returned, opening their store and post office, but this time a little north of the previous location, forming the nucleus of a new city called Leadville. Horace Tabor was not only the postmaster but the first mayor (re-elected for a second term) of this fast-growing city.

The Tabors lived for a time in a small clapboard cottage on Harrison Avenue. Later this house was moved to Carbonate Avenue, now known as East Fifth Street. This move was to make way for the Tabor Opera House, built in 1879. It was known as the "finest west of the Mississippi."

Horace Tabor was a kind and generous man who helped anyone in need. He grubstaked many miners and rarely received any benefits from these hand-outs. One day, however, a grubstake paid off. Two German shoemakers named August Rische and George Hook came into the Tabor store and asked Mr. Tabor for some mining supplies. Horace outfitted them with $60 worth of food and equipment they needed in their search for gold. They 'struck it rich' in the legendary Little Pittsburgh Mine. Mr. Rische and Mr. Hook sold out their interests to their benefactor, who became the sole owner and cleared between 1 and 1½ million dollars from the property.

This was the beginning of his wealth, as well as a new way of life. He later bought the fabulous Matchless and other mines in the Leadville area. Now a millionaire, he spent lavishly to build up Leadville into a first-class city. Lady Luck had certainly been with him, but had he not been willing to invest his money for the benefit of all the townspeople Leadville

27

Photo by Rocky Mountain View Co.

**The Tabor House in Leadville is now a tourist attraction.**

Photo by Evelyn E. Furman

**Mr. and Mrs. Clyde DuCharme in the living room of the Tabor House in Leadville.**

The living room of the Tabor House in Leadville.

A view of the dining room in the Tabor House.

One of the rare pictures of Augusta Tabor.

H.A.W. Tabor, the silver king of Colorado.

It was Tabor's kindness and generosity that led him to wealth and power.

N. Maxcy Tabor, son of Augusta and H.A.W. Tabor.

Photo courtesy J.P. Lester, Jr.

**Denver-Leadville Stage Coach. Nearly life size original painting was on walls of the Windsor Hotel. Photo taken just before Windsor was razed in 1960.**

**An early day prospector near Leadville.**

Sketch of the early Leadville, before being honored with a name.

California Gulch, where Abe Lee made the first gold discovery in the area.

Animated street scene in Leadville, winter of 1878-9. View west down lower Chestnut Street. Tabor's Bank in left foreground.

Leadville in its infancy, 1878. View from Brooklyn Heights.

**Early day Leadville, corner of Harrison Ave. and Chestnut St. Note the Little Church Saloon on east side.**

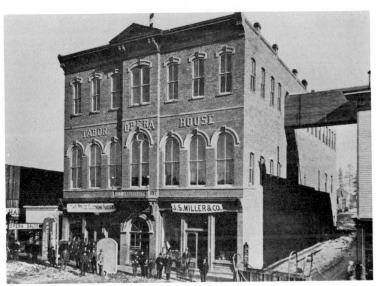

**The Tabor Opera House in Leadville.**

37

might easily have later become another ghost town, like so many that had been built on mining speculation. Thanks to H.A.W. Tabor, Leadville was to survive and prosper.

In 1880 the Tabors moved to Denver and Horace soon developed Denver into the Queen City of the West. Much of his capital went into building the first substantial structures in Denver. The Tabors themselves had a beautiful mansion at 17th and Broadway. He then constructed the Tabor building and the Tabor Grand Opera House, the most beautiful edifice in the West and a significant addition to Denver.

Later to become an important part of Tabor's life, Peter McCourt came to Colorado in 1873, lured by the mining boom. He settled in Leadville and became interested in properties there, and later in Cripple Creek and Victor. He met Tabor in Leadville and they established a close association lasting for many years, with Peter McCourt eventually becoming the manager of the Tabor Grand Opera House. He died in 1929.

Horace Tabor poured money into politics and supported the Republican Party almost single-handedly. The Lieutenant-governor of Colorado from 1879-1883, he served as a U.S. Senator in 1883, filling out the term of Senator Henry M. Teller who had been appointed Secretary of the Interior.

Horace and Augusta drifted apart and he eventually obtained a divorce—but against Augusta's will. She remained in the beautiful Broadway mansion and received a good part of the Tabor fortune in the divorce settlement. The scandal of the divorce and his subsequent marriage to Elizabeth McCourt (Baby Doe) in 1883 put an end to Mr. Tabor's political ambitions. In those days to divorce a faithful and good wife was considered an unpardonable sin.

Elizabeth McCourt Tabor was the mother of Lily and Silver. She was born in 1854, one of a family of 14 living in Oshkosh, Wisconsin. Possessing remarkable beauty, she was known as "the Belle of Oshkosh." She first married Harvey Doe (from a *good* Oshkosh family) and they moved west to seek their fortune, settling in Central City, Colorado. They worked at mining but without success, which was only one of their problems. Baby Doe (as she became known) wrote in her scrapbook about her son, stillborn July 13, 1979. Later,

Exterior view of the Tabor Grand Opera House in Denver, February 17, 1900.

Front Curtain, Tabor Grand Opera House. "So fleet the works of man, back to the earth again, ancient and holy things, fade like a dream."

39

View of Tabor Grand Opera House from the top balcony.

The Tabor Box in the Tabor Grand Opera House.

Souvenir of the Tabor Grand Opera House.

41

Denver Public Library Western Collection

**Home of H.A.W. and Augusta Tabor at 17th and Broadway. Photo by W.H. Jackson.**

Harvey and Elizabeth were divorced and Baby Doe was left without funds.

Jake Sands, a friend who had a clothing store first in Central City and later in Leadville, helped Baby Doe get to Leadville. It was not long before she managed to meet Horace Tabor in the Saddle Rock Restaurant near the Tabor Opera House. She had long dreamed of meeting this millionaire, and it seemed that Horace and Baby Doe were attracted to each other. It was said that it was love at first sight. Horace was then about 53 and Baby Doe was 29. Horace looked very distinguished to the former "Belle of Oshkosh."

When she first met him he was dressed in a dark suit with magnificent cuff buttons sparkling with diamonds and onyx, and wearing a large diamond ring. He had a look of honesty underneath his rugged features, and he possessed a generous and charitable manner that captivated Baby Doe. So it was that Baby Doe entered the life of H.A.W. Tabor—resulting in "The Tabor Triangle."

Many were sure that this beauty was only after Horace Tabor's money. Augusta, his hardworking first wife, had the sympathy of everyone and was loved by all in Leadville and Denver.

H.A.W. Tabor and Baby Doe announced their plans to marry. Horace, now a U.S. Senator, had the opportunity to stage an elaborate wedding in Washington. The date was set for March 1, 1883. Wedding invitations engraved in silver had quarter-inch silver borders. They were delivered by coachmen in a splendid Victoria. Rev. P.L. Chappelle of St. Matthews Catholic Church performed the ceremony. The wedding reception was held in the Willard Hotel in Washington, D.C.

Mrs. Nathaniel P. Hill, wife of the former senior senator from Colorado, sent her invitation back by the coachman. She had torn it into two pieces. Mrs. Teller, wife of a cabinet member, said, "Not for $10,000 would I have attended. I think it would have been an insult to the *real* Mrs. Tabor." Society did not accept Baby Doe and they always took Augusta's side. There were no women guests at the wedding except for Baby Doe's relatives.

Government figures, however, were in attendance: President Chester Arthur, his cabinet members and numerous senators and congressmen.

Baby Doe's wedding gown was of heavy brocaded white satin trimmed with marabow. The cost of the entire ensemble, including real lace lingerie, was $7,000. Even though it was her second marriage, she wore the traditional veil of orange blossoms.

Her wedding present from Horace was a $75,000 diamond necklace with the Isabella diamond. It reportedly was an authentic part of the jewels Queen Isabella had pawned to outfit Columbus for his voyage to America (the necklace failed to arrive from New York in time for the wedding). Elbow-length gloves completed her ensemble. She carried a bouquet of white roses.

All were hypnotized by this Irish beauty with large eyes of deep pansy hue. The Senator, with his strong, handsome features, looked distinguished in his dress suit with a white velvet waistcoat.

Baby Doe's relatives were all dressed in black—mourning for a passing relative.

Following the ceremony a supper table was laid, a colossal four-leaf clover at each end formed of red roses, white camellias and blue violets. Violets also encircled each guest's place at the table. Even the champagne buckets were decorated with garlands of flowers. A separate table with a canopy of flowers held the wedding cake. A massive bell of white roses was suspended over a great basin of flowers that added another three feet to the height of the cake. On top a heart of red roses was pierced by an arrow of violets shot from Cupid's bow of heliotrope. In each corner of the room was a bower of japonicas arranged to suggest the boxes of the Tabor Grand Opera House in Denver which the bridegroom had built.

The party lasted until midnight. Menu for the occasion: clear turtle soup, terrine de foies gras, broiled shad, capon, filet of beef, larded with mushrooms, canvas-back duck, omelet, souffle, wine with each course, brandy and chartreuse.

President Arthur, before leaving, asked for and received a rose from Baby Doe's bridal bouquet.

State Historical Society of Colorado

**Baby Doe Tabor, "the Belle of Oshkosh."**

Baby Doe—"All were hypnotized by this Irish beauty with large eyes of deep pansy blue."

Baby Doe dressed for winter in sealskin coat and cap.

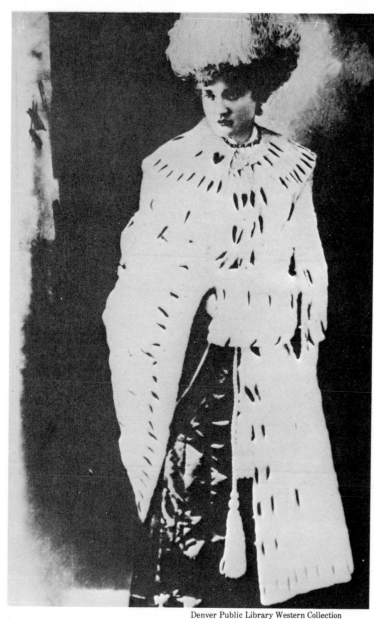

**Baby Doe was always a striking beauty.**

**A portrait of Baby Doe.**

When Baby Doe first met H.A.W. Tabor, she was 29 and he was
53.

Baby Doe's wedding gown was of heavy brocaded white satin trimmed with marabow. Her ensemble cost over $7,000.

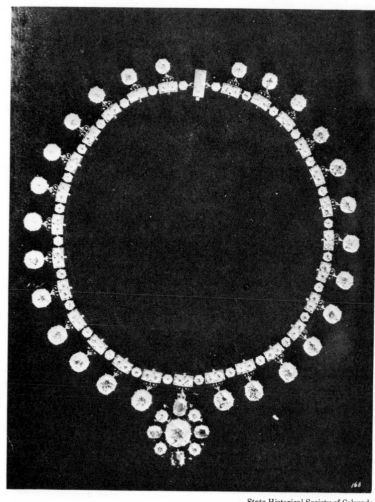

Tabor's gift to Baby Doe was a $75,000 diamond necklace with the Isabella Diamond.

H.A.W. Tabor and Baby Doe were married March 1, 1883. The reception was held at the Willard Hotel in Washington, D.C.

Thus did Horace Tabor marry this dazzling divorcee. The following day Father Chapelle learned that both Horace Tabor and his bride had been previously married and divorced. Incensed at what he considered a deception, Father Chapelle returned the $200.00 fee. Much to the surprise of all, Denver newspapers broke the story that Horace and Baby Doe had been secretly married Sept. 30, 1882 in St. Louis. This was three months before his divorce from Augusta was final. The Durango, Colorado, divorce and his marriage before the decree was final was a subject of much gossip.

After the wedding, the Tabors made their home in the Windsor Hotel in Denver. They had a very beautiful suite there until they moved into the mansion at 13th and Sherman Streets. The Denver *Times* of December 16, 1886 carried an article as follows: "Hon. H.A.W. Tabor purchased the handsome mansion and eight lots of Hon. Joseph Watson, located on the corner of Olive Street and Grant Avenue for $54,000. Mr. Tabor turned his Welton Street residence in as part payment at $12,000. This is said to be the largest sale of residence property ever made in the city."

Joseph Watson had built the mansion in 1880 in the best residential section of Denver. The plot extended from Sherman to Grant facing Thirteenth Avenue. There were beautiful gardens and a green lawn as soft as velvet. The lawn was elevated three feet from the street. A brownstone wall surrounded the entire property. Denverites were very impressed by this lovely setting for such a large and stately mansion. Beautiful statues and fountains caught the eye of those passing by. Peacocks were imported, at great cost, to give the yard the atmosphere of luxury, which was so dear to Mr. Tabor's heart.

The interior of this Victorian Mansion was a sight to behold. Woods used in the interior construction throughout were of the best walnut available. Beautiful wall-to-wall carpeting was all of floral design. Large crystal chandeliers were the finest and most expensive in Denver. Beautiful draperies and lace curtains made a perfect setting for the massive overstuffed living room furniture. Chairs and lounges gave a look of elegance. The wallpaper was one of the latest design. Mirrors with lovely gold frames added to the splendor of the rooms. Large pictures and paintings in costly gold frames graced the walls. The dining room had huge sideboards filled with expensive china and fancy dishes. There was one dinner set of richly encrusted blue and gold. The silver was the best to be had. There were gold-bowled spoons and many beautiful silver dishes of various description. Baby Doe saved some of these choice items, and they were found after her death in trunks stored in Denver.

There were two driveways from the carriage house and stable. Three beautiful carriages were ready at the Tabors' beck and call. One carriage was brown, trimmed with red, another was a blue enameled coach with thin gold lines painted around the body, and the other was a black carriage with white trimmings. Mr. Tabor had employed five stablemen, two drivers, and two footmen. He owned six horses, all well groomed. The horses had beautiful ornamental coverings and harnesses. It was an impressive sight to see these Tabor horses and carriages on Denver streets. The uniforms of the driver and footman were in harmony with the color scheme of the carriage and Baby Doe's dress. Baby Doe chose the carriage that matched what she wore on each occasion. At her side were her lovely little daughters wearing costly outfits, a frequent topic of conversation by Denverites. This mining man from the mountains startled Denverites with such displays of wealth. People gaped when the Tabor carriage drove by. Never had they seen such extravagance!

Baby Doe was always a striking beauty in her open carriage on Sixteenth Street or in the silk-lined box at the Tabor Grand Opera House. Often the eyes of the public were on Baby Doe, attracting as much attention as the famous stars appearing on stage. Years ago a lady in Leadville told the author that her mother, who lived in Denver, remembered seeing Baby Doe in her carriage. As the open carriage passed by, people were astonished and shocked to look up and see Baby Doe nursing her baby without any embarrassment whatsoever. It was not thought proper to nurse a baby in public in those days. This was one of many things for which Baby Doe was criticized.

Denverites questioned her character and said that she lacked refinement. Society continued to reject her.

Even though the ladies shunned her, they gazed with envy at her beautiful gowns and costly jewels. Baby Doe was well aware of her beauty and held her head high. She was a natural blonde, and Horace Tabor said her golden hair reached nearly to the floor when uncoiled.

H.A.W. Tabor and his family were now living a life of luxury. He was a politician, capitalist, and builder of a great empire. This was not to last. The Tabors did not long enjoy this beautiful mansion.

The downfall of H.A.W. Tabor and other millionaires came with the demonetization of silver, followed by the Panic of 1893. Congress repealed the Sherman Silver Act, so the government was no longer in the market for silver. The price dropped from $1.29 to 50¢ per ounce, less than the cost of mining it. Horace Tabor faced ruin. Now the gold standard men of the East had ruined the Western silver kings.

The Welton Street home of Horace Tabor and Baby Doe in
Denver.

The H.A.W. Tabor mansion at 13th and Sherman streets in Denver.

Interior of the Tabor mansion. Note picture of Lily Tabor at left.

Interior views of Tabor mansion. Note photo of Baby Doe in top picture, right.

Interior view of the Tabor mansion. Denverites had never seen such luxury.

One of the bedrooms in the Tabor mansion.

**Interior view of Tabor mansion. The baby carriage and high chair were the latest in design at the time.**

**Child's room in the Tabor mansion. Note large doll in the chair, toys on the floor.**

Another child's room in the mansion and a doll in the chair.

A rectangular bathtub was the height of splendor at that time.

Two more rooms in the lavish Tabor mansion.

## Chapter Three
# The Walls Came Tumbling Down

Tabor's wealth had vanished as quickly as it had appeared. His fortune was rapidly drained by unfortunate investments in foreign mining ventures that failed. He lost huge sums in South America and old Mexico. His reserves were gone and he had no funds to back up his many other businesses. He mortgaged his property and soon lost everything. Banks holding Tabor notes and mortgages were also caught in the disaster. Still believing that the Matchless would once again produce millions, Tabor never lost faith in the future.

Mr. and Mrs. Robert D. Elder (now deceased) were Leadville residents for many years, living in the older Elder family home at 310 W. 8th Street. A visit to the Elder home was always most enjoyable as they were interesting and likable people. Their home was furnished with many beautiful pieces and treasures from earlier days.

One day while the author was on a visit to this home, Mrs. Elder reminisced about her childhood days when her family lived in Denver near the Tabor mansion. She remembered the beautiful peacocks in the spacious yard. Mrs. Elder opened up her Bible and removed a small remnant of a gorgeous peacock feather. Holding it up for my inspection, she said, "Silver Dollar gave me this." It was a delight to see that she had so carefully saved this memento.

Mrs. Elder recalled when the Tabors lost the mansion, describing Mr. Tabor at their front door with suitcases in hand, removing the last of their personal belongings. What a sad time it was as they left the mansion forever.

Once again when visiting the Elder home the author listened with great interest while Mrs. Elder told another story of the Tabors. She said, "A wealthy man by the name of Tritch in the hardware business in Denver held many mortgages, and one was the Tabor mortgage on the mansion. It was a terrible blow to the Tabors to lose their beautiful home. The time had come for this mortgage holder to foreclose, and Mr. Tabor was so angered that he was going to shoot Mr. Tritch." Mrs. Elder continued, "My father, Mr. Hunter, was asked to stop Mr. Tabor from this act which would only get him into more trouble. My father said he would do it," she continued, "not so much for the sake of the mortgage holder, but for Mr. Tabor's sake—to keep him out of trouble." So with this turn of events, Mr. Hunter "saved the day," and prevented Mr. Tabor from carrying out the shooting. Mr. Hunter felt sorry for Mr. Tabor as he came out the front door of the mansion with the last two baskets filled with gold-framed pictures of his children and other family members.

After the Tabors left, there was no longer the well-kept yard. Tall grass had grown up all over the premises. Children were attracted to the spot as being a great place to play. Mrs. Elder, as a child, would go there and have a delightful time climbing on the statues left in the Tabor yard, especially the statues of the little fawns. Eventually the mansion was razed.

After the death of Baby Doe, the trunks in storage in Denver were opened. There were two pieces of stone found in an old satchel of cracking leather. A dusty tag on the handle of the satchel said, "Miss Tabor Hold." This was Silver Dollar. Perhaps Silver and her mother had rescued the stones from the old mansion at the time it was torn down. After the loss of the Tabor mansion in 1896, the family moved into a modest home on Tenth Street in West Denver.

# Chapter Four
## *Silver's Fantasy World*

Horace and Baby Doe had lived a life of luxury, but they both had known life without riches. The Tabor daughters had, until now, known only a life of luxury. They had difficulty adjusting to the sudden new life style.

Silver, as a child and even as a young girl in her early teens, lived in a make-believe world. When the family moved from the mansion in 1896, it was only a few days before Christmas. Silver wrote many letters to Santa Claus and her fairies at Sloans Lake in Denver. In learning to write, Silver's hand was guided by Lily or her mother. Therefore, her handwriting varies according to who helped her write each letter. Silver missed the expensive gifts she had been accustomed to receiving when the Tabors were wealthy. She quarreled with her sister, as children are apt to do. This worried Silver, causing her to think that might be the reason she had not received the presents she had requested in her letters to Santa Claus. She wrote repeatedly to Santa Claus and the fairies with a long list of her wants. Silver objected to the baths her mother insisted that she have, and worried about her behavior, writing the fairies to say she was sorry, begging not to be forgotten at Christmas.

After the death of Baby Doe Tabor, many of her trunks were still in storage in Denver. The contents, now the property of the Historical Society of Colorado, reveal much of interest concerning the Tabors. In the files are many of the Tabor letters that tell the story as the family lived it, including many of Silver's.

Silver writes the fairies from the Graymont Hotel, Denver. She is worried because she has not been good to her mother and Lillian, but hopes for Christmas presents and lists her wants for her birthday.

> *My own Darling Fairys*
>
> *Well darlings I will hope for the best and the best is presents from Santa Claus on Xmas which I am unworthy to receive on the account that I have talked and thought so badly of mamma to Lillian. How badly I feel and how ashamed I am of myself. My heart is breaking because of fear that I will be left out this Xmas which I could not stand. Last Xmas you didn't wake me up when you came and I felt so very badly about it but I know that if I am worthy to have you come to me I will also be allowed to see you come and help you trim my tree. If I have the grand heavenly joy of you and Santa Claus this Xmas I will stay up all night and take strong tea to keep me awake until you come and then I will have the joy of my life and will never again have [portion of letter illegible] of seeing you dearies. I will have a constant pain in my head until you come if you do. My brain and head will ache for fear you wont come. It will be a constant strain for 23 days until you may come. I wish that for my birthday present from you*
>
> > *2 willow rocking chairs in Blue*
> > *A nice mantle and grate*
> > *A blue velvet lounge with a Fairy sofa pillow on it*
> > *A large green shaded lamp*
>
> *If this furniture fits Mabella Edith I shall be much happier*

Letters of interest are as follows: A letter to Cupid (Lily) from her Aunt Emma (sister of Horace Tabor) reveals that the Tabors lived a short time in the Opera House.

> *My Darling Cupid,*
>
> *How do you like your new home in the Opera House? I was so very glad to get your letter. I wish your mamma was as good to write to me as you are. How are you getting along with your charm string? I will send you some mittens soon. I looked over the buttons at your cousin Willy the other day and picked out some for you. We have some snow on the ground. I wonder if you have, and if you are having any sleigh or sled rides. I suppose you are learning to read every day, and Silver is getting to talking quite plainly. Baby Fay tries to say everything and says some words very plainly and formed several words in sentences now. She calls me "Ga Ga" for Grandma. She is somewhat like*

PRIVATE AND PUBLIC BATHS          ELEVATOR

### THE GRAYMONT HOTEL
18TH AND CALIFORNIA STS.

STRICTLY FIRST CLASS SERVICE

RATES: $1.00, $1.50 AND $2.00 PER DAY

EUROPEAN PLAN

SPECIAL WEEKLY AND MONTHLY RATES

J. M. BENT, PROP.

PHONE 3043          DENVER, COLO., _____ 1903

My own Darling Fairys
Well darling I will hope
for the best and the best
is presents from Santa Claus
or Xmas which I am unworthy
to receive on the account that
I have talked and thought
so badly of mamma to Lillian.
How badly I feel and how
ashamed I am of my self.
My heart is breaking because
I fear that I will be left out
this Xmas which I could not
stand. Last Xmas you didn't
so wake me up when you came
and I felt so very badly
about it but I know that
if I am worthy & have you
come to me I will also be

allowed to see you come and
help you trim my tree. If I
have the grand heavenly
joy of you and Santa
Claus this Xmas I will
stay up all night and take
strong tea to keep me awake
until you come and then I
will have the joy of my
life and will never again have
~~the~~ ~~grand~~ ~~~~ ~~after~~ ~~that~~
of seeing you dearies. I will
have a constant pain in
my head until you come if
you do. My brain and head will ache
for fear you wont come
It will be a constant strain
for 23 days until you may
come. I wish that for my
birthday present from you

Parlor

2 willow rocking chairs in
Blue
A nice mantle and grate.
A blue velvet lounge with
a Fairy sofa pillow on it
A large green shaded lamp

If this furniture fits Mabells
Edith, I shall be much happier

71

*Silver. There is no such thing as keeping her still. I am so glad you keep well this winter and hope and pray no diptheria gets hold of you or Silver this winter. There has been a few cases in this town but I dont think there are any now.*

*I sent Silver a pair of stockings yesterday and have another pair begun. I want to knit a pair of mittens for Aunt Tryphena and her twin sister Maria also, before Christmas, not forgetting your little hands either. Dear Cupid, write auntie again. I am so glad to get letters from anybody I love so much as I do your own dear little self. I would dearly love to see you, but cannot be in two places at once. My room here is so very comfortable that it is nice to be here in it. So please accept much love and many kisses from Aunt Emma and kiss papa and mamma and Lilian many times for me, and remember me to your Grandma and aunts Lillie and Claudia.*
*Your loving Aunt Emma.*

Horace Tabor and Peter McCourt are busy with the mining projects in Mexico. A letter to Lily from her Uncle Pete.

*Jesus Maria, Mexico*
*Sept. 23, 1893*
*Darling Lillie:*
*Papa & I are having a lovely time here but if Mama Honeymaid & you were only with us then it would be fun. We are coming home in a few days. We will then tell you all about our trip on the stage, the mules, how we slept outdoors and on the floors of the houses on the way & what fun it was. The next time we come here we will take you all & you can ride a burro. Kiss Mama Honeymaid, Grandma Claudia & all for Papa & I.*
*Papa has something nice for you from Mr. Hart.*
*Your loving uncle*
*Pete*

Another letter to Lily from Uncle Pete.

*Trinidad 26/11/93*
*Dearest Lillie:*
*Papa and I are here together and only have a few minutes to get a mouthful to eat and send you our love. You dont know how much we love you. Nobody knows how much we love you. Just as soon as we get the money we will telegraph Mama and will meet you at Nogales. We are going to get a little mule for you to ride with Honeymaid.*

My Darling Cupid,

How do you like your new home in the Chine House? I was so very glad to get your letter. I wish your mamma was as glad to write to me as you are. How are you getting along with your charm string? I will send you some buttons soon. I looked over the buttons at your cousin Will's the other day and picked out some for you. We have some snow on the ground. I wonder if you have, and if you are having any sleigh or sled rides. I suppose you are learning to read every day, and Silver is getting to talking quite plainly. Baby Fay tries to say every thing and says some words very plainly, and connects several words in sentences now. She calls me "Ga Ga", for Grandpa. She is somewhat like Silver. There is no such thing as keeping her still. I am so glad you keep well this winter and hope and pray no diphtheria gets hold of you or Silver this winter. There has been a few cases in this town, but I don't think there are any now.

I sent Silvan a pair of stockings yesterday, and have another pair begun. I want to knit a pair of mittens for aunt Tryphena, and her twin sister Maria also, before Christmas, not forgetting your little hands either. Dear Rupert, write auntie again. I am so glad to get letters from any body I love so much as I do your own dear little self. I should dearly love to see you, but can not be in two places at once. My room here is so very comfortable that it is home to me to be here in it. So please accept much love and many kisses from aunt Emma, and kiss papa and mamma and Silvan many times for me, and remember me to your Grandma and aunts Lillie and Claudie.

Your loving Aunt Emma.

*What do you think of that. Give Papa's and my love to
Mama Honeymaid, Grandma Claudia and all.*
*Your Loving Uncle*
*Pete*

Silver writes her darling fairies and Santa Claus. "Be sure
and don't fail to wake me before you go."

*My own darling Fairys and Santa Claus—*
*When you are through fixing my Xmas tree and have
fixed everything wake me up so that I can see you and talk
to you and ask you what I want to about yourselves and
where you live and about anything. Silver*
*Be sure and don't fail to wake me up before you go and let
me see you all. Love—Silver.*

1896. Another letter to Santa Claus with a long list of her
wants for Christmas.

*St. Nickolas*                          *Sunday Dec 1896*
*Darling Santa Claus*
*I love you so much. Please bring me four tiny lead
pencils, box of beautiful handkerchiefs for my-self, some
little cooking dishes, some little eating dishes, a dosan little
spoons, a dosan little knives, a dosan little forks, a little
trunk with a key for my-self a foot & a half long a foot tall
one " wide, some candy, a nice little tight woden box, a book
that tells all about Heavens, oceans, a watched trimmed in
blue & yellow for me, a little pair of sissors sharp pointed,
a little bit of a Karosine lamp, three spools of common
Fairie thread, three spools of rich Fairie silk thread, a
little Silver Gold & all color paper, some Fairie Valintines,
a Fairie doll a Fairie bedstead, some Fairie chairs,
Fairie cup & saucer, a finger nail cleaner for my-self
trimmed with Aubys & Turquoise, a box of all color glass
bottles that I cannot break, a book of Xmas, one small play
lamb, one play rabbit, some canes of candy, a little tiny
library, a little looking glass, a little square plater [a little
bottle of purple ink, four little pens], some spools of all color
silk ribbons, a little ring of keys, a deck of round &
heart cards, a green frog with a white breast, a box powder
for my dollie & paint, a back hair pin for my dollie, some
writting paper for my-self, a baby doll that talks and opens
& closes its eyes.*
*List of clothes and other things for it*
*3 night gowns*

*a nice little pair of comfortable slippers*
*A nice little dollies bed*
*A little eye shade*
*Some little Jewelry*
*A pair of bracelets in red blue & yellow*
*" necklace of each color*
*" breast pin    "        "*
*" little comb trimmed in each color*
*" set of hair pins for her*
*" dollies desk*
*" dress for her of this shade of blue, long party low neck*
*short sleves, sample inclosed.*
  *dress of this kind of white style same blue, sample*
*inclosed.*
  *dress of white satin party style same blue.*
  *dress of the shade of Salmon high neck, long and*
*[illegible] sleeves, a beautiful pair of glass ball slippers, a*
*beautiful pair of pink silk stockings. Love & kisses to you &*
*Fairies*

*Lovingly*
*Silver Tabor*

Silver continues her letters to her Fairies, revealing her jealousy concerning Lily, apparently increasing with the loss of the family fortune.

*My Own Darlings*
  *You are certainly the only ones that realize the heart-aches that I go through. How parshall mamma is on Lily. Mamma does not care how much I see Lily wearing diamonds and when I tell her that the safety pin does not belong to Lily anymore than it does to me—because we both wore it when we were young—I told her that in the eyes of God it doesnt but she says that it does. You know that I ask mamma for very little and Lily would spend 50 cents a day on foolishness. If mamma tries to advise with her as all mothers do she roasts her and at every word that doesnt please her she storms around like a wild bull. I am able to stand no more of her. There is nothing pious about her and I am getting to almost hate her. Mamma is breaking my hear with parshiality and Lily reads novels all the time. She is as extravagent as she can be and the other day I told her not to buy novels as they were 10 or 15 cents and that stockings were only 10 cents and mamma could not aford to buy them for herself even at that rate and she snapped back*

*at me that she ought to have a book if she wanted it and she went out and bought it. Xmas is nearly here and in Leadville I have a letter to you of what I want. Have the Fairys up in Leadville go up into our room and into my box that came out of our trunk and down in among my things in it is the letter telling what I want. If you cannot do this please let me know at once and I will write a new letter of what I want. I know and realize to my great grief and shame and sorrow and my utmost regret that I sinned most terriably around Easter time—1903. Had I it to do over God knows and you do too that I would not do it again. You can never realize what sorrow* [rest of letter missing].

Silver writes to her fairy Ellabella, in Fairyland, Sloans Lake—asks for presents. She signs the letter Concuella Grace Tabor, 833 Broadway

*My Own Dear Ellabella My Guard,*

*I love you so much Darling, I hope to have my ball soon for I long for it. I want you to get me the smalast ball you can get in the city two and bring me the things you have got for me as soon as you posabaly can. Dear Ellabella please write me a little letter as soon as you can and tell me just what you want me to do and I will keep your letter with me all the time and when ever I forget I will read it again and again.*

*My Guard, I hope you are not mad at me, pet. [Where are my two cats we canot find them and pet them for me and all you do is just to get them without a word and I will write them a letter and roast them and make them jump out of their shoes.* (Author note: Impossible to decipher)*].*

*Well Dearest, next to mah and sis you are the sweetest friend on earth I have met or found. I will plant the bleading-heart and the heliotrope and ruffled panseys if you will only order them to be sent to the house and pay for them. The rest I will do. I hope you will receive this letter and I will receive one from you.*

> *Lovingly your own friend*
> *Concuella Grace Tabor*
> *833 Broadway*
> *March 1, 1908*
> *With love to all the faires. Councella Tabor*

Another letter to Ellabella—wants a big ball, signs her letter Silver Dollar Tabor.

*Darling Ellabella,*

*I love you so much. I wrote to aunt Claudia Tuesday, hope she is well. Lily wrote to grandma today but did not send it. I spoze as you know Mr. Jurard was here Wedsday. Come Ellabella bring me a big ball. Sophie was hear today and I made a hood for my doll. I have no news to tell for you know everything. For my sake if you love me write me very soon. My flowers will bloom soon won't they. I haven't mor to say.*

*Lovingly,*
*Silver Dollar Tabor*
*July 24, Wednesday*

Darling Santa Claus
I love you so much,

Please bring me four tiny bad pirate
a box of beautiful handkerchiefs for
my-self, some little cooking dishes,
some little eating dishes, a dozen
little spoons, a dozen little knives
a dozen little forks a little trunk
with a key for my-self a foot
& a half long a foot tall one " wide
some candy, " nice little tight
woden box, a book that tells all
about Heavens sceans, a watch
trimmed in red blue & yellow for
me a little pair of sissiors &
sharp pointed, a little bit of a
Harosine lamp, three spools of

79

common Fairie thread three spools
of rich " silk thread, a little
Silver Gold & all color paper some
Fairie Valintines, a Fairie doll
a " ~~bead~~ bedstead some " chairs
" cup + saucer, a finger nail
cleaner for my- self trimmed with
Aubys & Turqurse, a box of all
color glass bottles that I cannot
breaks a book of X has one small
play lamb one play rabbit, some
canes of candy, a little tiny
Library a little looking glass,
a little square ploter ~~a little~~
~~bottle of purple ink four little~~
~~pens~~, some spools of all color silk
ribbons, a little ring of keys
a deck of round + heart cards
" green frog with a white breast
a box powder for my dollie & paint
" back hair pin for my dollie
some ~~wool~~ ~~paper~~
writting paper for my- self
a baby doll that talks & opens
& closes its eyes
Dist of ~~the~~ clothes for it & other *& other things*

3 night gowns
a nice little pair of comfortables
slippers,
A nice nice little dollies bed.
" little eye shade
some little Jewelry
a pair of bracelets in red blue & yellow
" neck lace of each color
" breast pin " " " in each color
" little comb trimmed in each color
" ett " of hair pins for her
" dollies desk
" dress for her of this shade of blue
long party low neck short sleeves
sample inclosed
dress of this kind of white style same blue
sample inclosed
dress of white satin party style same
blue
dress of the shade of Salmon high neck
long & long sleeve a beautiful pair of
glass ball slippers a " " pair of pink silk
stockings

Love & kisses to you & Fairies

Lovingly

Silver Tabor

81

My own Darlings

You are certainly the only ones that realize the
heart aches that I go through. How harsh all is mama
is on Lily. mamma does not care how much I see
Lily wearing diamonds and when I tell her that the
sapphire pin does not belong to Lily anymore than it
does to me — because we both wore it when we were
little — I told her that in the eyes of God it doesn't
belong — I told her that it does. Gertrude that I go if
but she says that it does. Gertrude that Lily would spoil
me. For every little thing mamma tries to abuse
me. Every single hour. If mamma tries to abuse
her as all mothers do she roasts her all the day
and it doesn't please her she tries to abuse her,
she wants to full, if I am able to stand in most
there is nothing to come to it her and I am getting without
is with mamma is breaking my heart with partiality and
she spends money all the time she is so extravagant as she
can. I and the other day I told her not to buy my dress as
they were 13 or 15 I and that stockings were only 10g and
mamma could not afford to buy them for her and even
I was so and she snapped back at me that she
ought to have a book if she wanted it. and she
went out and bought it. Xmas is nearly here and
in Leadville I have a letter to you I what I
want Have the Fairys up in Leadville go up
into our room and into my box that came
out of our trunk and down in among my
things in it are is the letter telling
what I want. If you

## Chapter Five
# *Death of a Giant*

By the turn of fortune's wheel, Mr. Tabor's wealth had vanished, but this did not discourage him. He was determined to make another strike. He was back searching for gold just as he had done in 1859. Even though now much older, he was not afraid of hard work and was prospecting at Boulder. He tried to get Winfield Scott Stratton, the Cripple Creek millionaire, to invest in his new venture. He was not successful, but Mr. Stratton did help in giving Mr. Tabor ten $1,000 bills. "Make use of it as you want," said Mr. Stratton, "and if you can ever conveniently return it, do so. If not don't consider there is any obligation in the matter."

This Boulder mining venture failed because of lack of capital. The money ran out before he could reach the ore. After all his work, Mr. Tabor was disappointed in not being able to continue until he was successful in striking it rich once more. Still, Mr. Tabor and his wife had faith in the future.

Some of the women who had always sided with Augusta predicted that Baby Doe would soon leave Mr. Tabor. After all, he was old and had no money. Baby Doe, with her beauty, was certain to seek greener pastures. Not so. She was willing to part with her jewels and finery to finance the family needs and debts. She remained with Horace and helped him in every way possible.

In 1897 the family moved to Ward, Colorado. Horace labored trying to develop his Eclipse Mine. The family lived in a small house with a lean-to. It was located on the property near the shaft house and dump. After life in the city Silver was delighted with the beautiful scenery and the wide open spaces.

She loved animals and liked being around the cow, the horse and the cats that the family had acquired. She thought it great fun to make friends with the pine squirrels and watch the birds.

But this mining venture was another in Tabor's line of failures.

The next move was back to Denver and living in a cheap, two room suite at the Windsor Hotel. It was nothing like the elaborate suite Horace and Baby Doe had there after their fashionable Washington wedding. This was where Baby Doe and Horace had started life together. Strange how it was destined to be their last home together.

Senator Walcott used his influence to get Horace Tabor appointed Postmaster of Denver by President William McKinley. The people of Denver were pleased to have Mr. Tabor as their postmaster, and felt that he surely deserved it. After all, he had given the government a large plot of valuable land in Denver on which to erect this post office, and had practically supported the Republican party when the political leaders were badly in need of funds.

Mr. Tabor gave up his mining ventures forever. He was content with his new position and settled down to living at the Windsor. Here he had a magnificent view of the Rocky Mountains to the West, and beyond that the vivid memory of his beloved Leadville home and mines that had brought him millions.

Tabor, now with a regular income as postmaster, agreed to let his family go to New York to see if the change of climate would help Lily. It was thought she had catarrh. Baby Doe suffered from neuralgia. While in New York, Lily and Silver were determined to sell an Indian bone (dug up by Horace while mining) to a museum, convinced it must have great historical value.

Baby Doe and the girls remained in the City from December 1898 to March 1899, living in a small room they rented for $20.00 a month.

Silver, or Honeymaid as she was fondly called by her family, wrote to her Papa, thanking him for his registered letter which included $20.00:

*My own darling papa. I love you soo much. Your registered
letter came to day with 20 dollars in it. So glad because
Lily left her other blue ring in the baker store last night for
bread. We will [get] it today. I want to live here but you
must come and live with me. Cannot live away from you
my dear sweet papa. I was soo glad to go in to a meat
market. I saw the two hind legs of a cow. I was never in a
meat-market before. I am having lots of fun and I would
make you have just as much fun as I do. Lots of kisses from
Lily and your own loving baby.*

*Honeymaid*

Horace had not been feeling very well and was pleased when
the family returned. His health continued to deteriorate. After
a sudden attack of pain Tabor called on his doctor who
diagnosed his condition as appendicitis. But due to his
advanced age and weakened condition it was decided not to
operate. Shortly after, H.A.W. Tabor died on April 10, 1899,
with Baby Doe at his bedside. Also at his bedside were Maxcy,
Lily (age 15), and Silver (age 9).

Thus the curtain fell on the life of H.A.W. Tabor, ending a
fantastic and colorful American saga. His life had left its
mark on Leadville and Denver as well as the nation's capital.
His beginning was at the foot of the ladder. Led by
determination and his special talents, he reached the stars, if
only for a moment.

The day Tabor was buried flags were flown at half-mast
throughout Colorado. His was the finest funeral ever held in
Denver. Among the hundreds of floral tributes, the most
outstanding one came from Leadville. Made of American
Beauty roses, it was shaped in the form of a cornucopia. This
creation was six feet high and most impressive, a touching last
tribute from the people of Leadville to H.A.W. Tabor! They
had not forgotten, after all, that in life he had provided from
his magic cornucopia an abundance of wealth for Leadville.
That symbol will undoubtedly remain synonymous with the
Horace Tabor mystique for years to come. Truly, he was "Mr.
Leadville."

H.A.W. Tabor was buried in Calvary cemetery, Denver.
This cemetery, years later, was abandoned and all graves
moved. The property was sold, and now is the location of

Botanic Gardens. Part of the stone marking the Tabor grave in Calvary Cemetery was torn from its foundation and was later found a long distance from the grave. Weeds and grass had overrun all the graves. Later Mr. Tabor's body was moved to Mount Olivet cemetery.

Augusta, Horace's first wife, it was said, died of a broken heart. She had received a good part of the Tabor fortune in the divorce settlement and had invested it wisely. She moved to Pasadena, California, where she died on February 1, 1895. She was the first of the Tabor triangle to die. Their son Maxcy had her body brought to Denver for burial in Riverside cemetery. She left a considerable estate, willing half to Maxcy and half divided equally between her brothers and sisters.

Maxcy Tabor lived a quiet life in Denver, managing the Tabor Grand Opera House, and later the Windsor and Brown Palace Hotels, residing at the Brown for a time. Their daughter, Persis Augusta Tabor, was born while the family was living there. Maxcy died at age 71 in his home at 1120 Grant Street in Denver.

Grateful Denverites presented a medallion to H.A.W. Tabor at the opening of his $700,000 Tabor Grand Opera House in Denver. At the bottom is a bucket of ore picks and shovels to show the beginning of Tabor's prospecting. Next above is the old Tabor store in Oro, near Leadville. In the center is the Tabor Block, and at the top the Tabor Grand Opera House. Ladders on each side show how he climbed to success.

Horace Tabor and his family were very proud of this beautiful and elaborate watch fob depicting his beginning at the bottom of the ladder and on up to the top. Silver and her mother vowed they would never part with this, and for a long time it was kept at the Hamilton National Bank in Denver. Found among the effects after Baby Doe's death, it is now on display in the Colorado State Historical Society. Here is Silver Dollar's letter concerning the watch fob:

*Leadville, Colo., May* [date missing]

*To the*
*President and Mr. Weckbach,*
*Hamilton National Bank,*
*Denver, Colo.*

*Gentlemen:*
    *Please have Papa's gold fob placed in my mother's (Mrs.*
*E.B. Tabor) name as it belongs to her and she will pay the*
*principal and interest when it is due.*
    *Papa left it to her with the estate.*
    *Please pardon paper—I am on the mine.*
    *We both send our deep appreciation and kindest regards*
*to you all.*

*Very sincerely,*
*Silver Dollar Tabor*

**Watch fob presented to H.A.W. Tabor on
opening night at Tabor Grand Opera House.**

A portrait (in color) of H.A.W. Tabor.

The Tabors moved from the mansion to a more modest residence.

As financial woes worsened, the Tabors moved into this small house on Denver's north side.

The funeral procession for H.A.W. Tabor made its slow journey from the capitol to Sacred Heart Church and to its final destination, Mt. Calvary Cemetery.

## Chapter Six
# *The Matchless Lives On*

Baby Doe and her two daughters now faced life without their revered provider. For a time they lived at 833 Broadway and rented rooms at the Garymont Hotel at 18th and California. In 1902 they moved to Leadville, living in a modest place on West Seventh Street.

Baby Doe remembered Horace Tabor's dying words, "Hang on to the Matchless—it will pay millions again." This is exactly what Baby Doe intended to do. The Matchless Mine is located about a mile east of downtown Leadville. Living in Leadville, it would be easier to get the mine operating again.

Silver enjoyed life up in the mountains, but Lily was not satisfied with this life style at all. She felt it was too difficult for her mother to try to get the Matchless "paying" again. Baby Doe and her daughters worked hard trying to make a living with this mining venture. Baby Doe soon found out it was not easy, but kept trying to interest others in investing in the Matchless. Through the years, she was often involved with court cases over the mine. The Tabor family finally moved up to the shack at the mine. It was only a one-room building with a lean-to on the west end. It wasn't well suited to rear her daughters, but it saved paying rent and besides that, living near the mine she felt she could guard it properly. She kept a shotgun handy to scare off intruders. The daughters had been born into a life of luxury, and Lily, especially, grew tired of this dull life. At 18 years of age, she wanted to go elsewhere, and did convince Baby Doe to spend winters in Denver, and the summers in Leadville.

In addition to cabins and shacks, there were once many fine homes around the Leadville mining area. The Matchless mine in those days was not the lonely place that it is now. There were neighbors close by living at the other mines. After the big boom of the early days there continued to be activity in the Leadville mining area. The Matchless, and other mines, had many buildings with various uses. The railroads built branches up to the mines and hauled cars of ore from the mines to the smelter. In the beginning the grocery stores would make regular deliveries to the residents. Wagons were used, and the delivery men often took riders on their way up the gulches. Baby Doe frequently had rides up to the Matchless with her supply of groceries. Silver enjoyed her friends around the Matchless, and they had good times together. Leadville suburbs had schools and the usual business establishments, and there were always saloons. [Author's note: when I came to Leadville in 1933, there were still fine clapboard houses far up the mountain near the Resurrection mine. They were by then unoccupied and deteriorating. The Rio Grande Railroad still made trips to the mines to pick up cars of ore, and hauled them to the Arkansas Valley Smelter. Most of these buildings have been torn down and the people are gone. There is little remaining to reveal the location of those interesting places. Likewise most of the mine buildings have been demolished—with only the mine dumps remaining to mark the location.]

Baby Doe, Lily and Silver, when working in the mine, had some bad experiences at times. They felt God worked a miracle, preventing Baby Doe from falling down the mineshaft, as this letter from Baby Doe, Lily and Silver tends to verify.

*Leadville—Dec. 29—1906*

*My Darling Teacher and Family*

*We wrote our beloved Father Guida and sent it by express. He should have received it the day after but not hearing from him we fear he did not. Please let him read this letter. We hope you are all well. Expect to see you soon. We want the dear Father to read the following. He was so wonderful. God worked a great miracle [portion of letter destroyed] twenty eighth day of November Mamma was working down the mine with the windlass. A man by the name of Atkins was on the other side of it. They were*

*hoisting rock from a shaft sixty five feet deep, that was two
hundred and forty-four feet underground where they were.
They would lower the buckets down sixty five feet to a man
by name of Wilbur Simmons who would fill them and they
would pull them up. Mr. Atkins took the bucket of rock and
dragged it some thirty feet through the drift and mamma
would let out the rope for him. She was silently praying to
Saint Anthony and Saint* [Expdit] *for strength when Mr.
Atkins suddenly called to her* [this is the kind of stuff you
are looking for, come see this bucket!] *She walked over
and as she came near the open shaft she received such a
terrible blow in the forhead that it knocked her backwards
right on top of the open shaft. She* [portion of letter
destroyed] *her heavy body going down and screamed
terribly for she knew that the man underneath her would be
instantly killed. Mr. Atkins was so horror struck that he
could not move. He could see her going down fast. Mamma
was lifted right out of that hole and placed on the boards
beside it and no one knows who did it or how it was done
but we know that it was our blessed Saviour. She was
unharmed and not a sign of pain or soreness was on her
forhead where she was struck that mighty blow and no sign
of it or bad effects in any way except that for many nights
she would wake up thinking she was going down that hole.
After she was lifted out of the hole she finished her days
work of many hours and was perfectly well. Mamma told
me that it was Satan that* [portion of letter destroyed]
*because he cannot harm* [portion of letter destroyed] *way
and had anything else struck her such a heavy blow there
would have been signs of it on her forhead but it was as
smooth and white as ever. She said he knows we are going to
save the mine and wants to kill me but God in His mercy
has attended with mighty Angels all through this battle.
May God bless and keep you all. With a word of love from
mamma Lily and your loving*
                    *Honeymaid*
*P.S. My Darling Ones. Please excuse lead pencil. There is
no ink where I am as I am in Leadville.*

In 1902 Baby Doe with her daughters went to Wisconsin and
Chicago to visit her relatives. This delighted the daughters
and Lily wanted to stay. Baby Doe's mother was ill, and the
relatives pleaded with Baby Doe to let Lily stay at least until

Leadville - Dec -29- 1906

My Darling Teacher and Family

We wrote our beloved
Father Guida and sent it by express.
He should have received it the day
after but not hearing from him we
fear he did not. Please let him read
this letter. We hope you are all well.
Expect to see you soon. We want the
dear Father to read the following. It
was wonderful. God worked a great
miracle. ... twenty sixth day of
... mine was working down
the mine the Sunddass. A man by
the name Atkins ... in the ...
out of it. ... ... ... back from
a shaft ... fifty feet deep, ...
two hundred and forty four feet
underground when they were. They
would lower the buckets down sixty
four feet to a man by name of
Wilbur Simmons who would fill

her grandmother recovered. Baby Doe finally agreed. Baby Doe's brother Steve wrote Baby Doe on October 10, 1902:

*HINCH'S RESTAURANT*
*618 Minnesota Avenue.*
*Kansas City, Kansas, Oct. 10, 1902*
*My Darling Sister and Sweet Hon,*
*How glad I was to get your letter, it has been so long since I have had a letter from anyone, I am still here, but how I wish I were back in Denver. Now Lizzie I am going to see you for I have made up my mind to beat my way, I know it will be a hard trip and will take me some time but I will make it, I hardly make my living here, I will start in 10 or 15 days.*

*I am so glad you went to Chicago and you will be glad that you left dear Lily as it will do a world of good and Lizzie, it is real noble and brave in you as I know just how you worry. But God will take the best of care of her. With barels of Love to you both & Lily. When you write. Your affct. bro. & Uncle Steve, address 618 Minnesota Ave.*

In a letter to Silver Dot writes that they miss her. "There is no one to 'chuck-chuck' now."

*Sunday*

*My dearest Silver:*
*We were so sorry not to see you before you went back. But we expect to see you again soon. Remember! It's so nice to have Lily here that I guess we can't let her go back.*

*Next time you come will look out that you don't get away from us so soon. We'll know how you act and will watch you closely.*

*It's so nice to have all the relatives so close to us instead of way way down there.*

*I went with Claud and Andrew to see Lily last night. She's looking so well. No one would guess she'd been so sick.*

*How are you and Aunt Lizzie. I miss you so. There is no one to "chuck-chuck" now though and so I'm not teased.*

*Grandma is well and happy. Papa & Madeline have gone over to see her but I had so many letters to write I stayed at home.*

*How is your doll? Can she wear her "poke" now or isn't it the style.*

95

Kansas City, Kansas, Oct 10 1902

My Darling Sister & Sweet Hun

How glad I was to
get your letter, it has been so long
since I have had a letter from
anyone, I am still here, but how I wish
I were back in Denver. Now Lizzie I am
going to see you for I have made up
my mind to beat my way, I know
it will be a hard trip & will take
me some time but I will make it, I
hardly make my living here, I will start
in 10 or 15. days. I am so glad you went
to Chicago & you will be glad that you
left dear Lily as it will do a World of
good & Lizzie it is real Noble & Brave in
you as I know full how you worry, But
God will take the best of care of her
With Barrels of Love to ~~Both~~ You Both
+ Lily when You write Your Affch Bro
+ Hinch Stine. adress 618 Minnesota Ave

96

Sunday.

My dearest Silver:-

We were
so sorry not to see you
before you went back.
But we expect to see
you again soon. Remember!
It's so nice to have Lily
here that I guess we
can't let her go back.
Next time you come we'll
look out that you don't

get away from me so soon.
I'll know how you act and
will watch you closely.
It's so nice to have all the
relatives so close to us instead
of way way down there.
I went with Claud and Andrew
to see Lily last night. She's looking
so well. No one would guess
she'd been so sick.
How are you and Aunt Lizzie
I miss you so. There is no one
to "chuck-chuck" now though
and so I'm not teased.
Grandma is well and happy.
Papa & Madeline have gone over
to see her but I had so many
letters to write I stayed at home
How is your doll? Can she wear her

"poke" now or isn't it
the style.

Stella went home - that
is back to Fond du Lac
yesterday - Last Sunday
Vol was here and he was
so sorry not to see you
+ Aunt Lizzie.

Be a good girl + don't
"chuck" anyone.

With love from all to you
and Aunt Lizzie

Affetimately
Dot -

*Stella went home—that is home to Fond du Lac yesterday. Last Sunday Vol was here and he was so sorry not to see you & Aunt Lizzie.*

*Be a good girl & don't "chuck" anyone.*

*With love from all to you and Aunt Lizzie.*

*Affectionately,*
*Dot*

Time goes on and Lily writes that she likes being left with her grandmother and Claudia. In another letter she wrote, "Claudia says she thinks Silver was as beautiful a thing as anyone could see that last day in the car. She says you can't have me."

Baby Doe and Silver are anxious for Lily to return home. Lily again writes, "Kiss dear Silver for me and remember that I will come as soon as I can—Bushells of love from your Lily."

Later Lily writes her mother, "I am very sad not to obey you at once but you will see how it is when you get this. Please forgive me for all and try to let me stay until Claudia is well."

Lily writes that her grandmother is much better and talking a little more plainly. Hopes she regains full speech. She says Claudia and Baby are feeling well. They look forward to another visit from Baby Doe and Silver. Lily needs a coat and her teeth filled.

*My Own Darlings,*

*It is an eternity since we have heard from you—but are hoping every mail to get a letter. Dear Grandma is much better and is talking a little more plainly. Oh! will she ever regain her full speech. The Baby and Claudia are feeling well and so things are looking a little brighter, but we won't be happy till you are both with us, won't it be grand, a grand good time together—my dear ones.*

*I hope all is well at the Mine and that you are safe and well—I know what a struggle you are having and it just seems awful that you can have no rest—and now I want a coat and I want to have my tooth refilled with gold for the other filling is not satisfactory and if you can send me a little money I will buy a coat and a few necessities and have my tooth fixed. But don't do it if it will be hard, for I can get along & wish I could help you instead of sending for money. I wish I could send it to you instead.*

100

*Write more often and Heaps of Love*
*From your Lily.*
*Love from all.*
*Grandma is so happy that you are coming to her.*

Lily writes Baby Doe, offering to send her jewelry if she needs money. Baby Doe's illness worries Lily.

*My Darling,*
*You can never know how sad I felt or how terribly worried I was and am over you being sick. I was afraid you would be—after that storm. We just got back from Church and how I prayed that you are well by this time. I hope and pray that I will get a letter from you to-morrow. Oh! I know how I have acted, how ungrateful and hateful I've been but I know I would die from sorrow if anything should happen to either of you. But God will be merciful to even me and make and keep you well and strong but I am awfully worried about you. I sent the letter you enclosed to Mr. Mills and I will do the other things you told me to—everyone shall think you are in Columbus, Ohio. Now do be careful and take care of yourself and don't try to do any business or go out until you are perfectly well for you might take more cold. A person is susceptible to the cold when they have one and it is dangerous to take more. I wish you would have your meals taken to your room for a little while for it is dangerous to sit in the restaurant and then go out into the cold. We found that out at the Home Dairy. It would be much better to have them sent to your room and as far as the expense it will be far better in the end and pay you for you will be well twice as quick, and do cover your chest up well with your coat so you won't get pneumonia. Do these things for me Darling—*
*Silver dear, please write me and tell me just how Mamma feels and if she needs me or if I could do any good. I will come at once for I could get there by borrowing money on my jewelry. I wish you had taken it with you and don't worry about money for if you get short one little bit, just telegraph to me and I will send the jewelry to you at once, in the Wells Fargo or any place you want. If you didn't send for it I would never forgive you, Dearest. Now **don't** forget to send for it. Will you—Tell me, Honey, where Mama's cold is. Is it in her lungs. Oh! I hope she is alright by* [rest of letter missing]

My Own Darlings

It is an eternity
since we have heard
from you - but all hoping
every mail to get a letter -
Dear Grandma is much
better and is talking a little
more plainly - Oh! will
she ever regain her full
speech - The Baby and
Claudia all feeling well
and so things all looking
a little brighter, but
we wont be happy till

My Darlings

You can never know
how sad I felt or how terribly
worried I was and am
when I over you being
sick. I was afraid you
would be—after all that
storm. We just got back
from Church and how
I prayed that you are
well by this time. I hope
and pray that I will get
a letter from you to-morr-
Ow! I know how I have
acted how ungrateful and
hateful I've been but
I know I would die from
sorrow if any thing should
happen to either of you
but god will be merciful

Lily always had an excuse for not returning home to Baby Doe and Silver. They were shocked to get a letter from Lily postmarked May 15, 1908. It was written on printed stationery from Marshall Field and Company—Chicago. Lily writes:

*My Dear Ones,*

*I was married yesterday to the best man in the world, and I can not tell you how happy I am. If you knew how good he is you would be happy with me, and I want you to love him, not only for my sake, but because he is so fine and I tell you, darlings—I would never have been happy without him. We both send you heaps of love, Your Loving daughter, Lily.*

*It is almost two months since I have heard from you— what is the matter? P.S. Claudia did not know that we were to be married until after we were married, so she had nothing to do about it, don't blame her.*

The return address was J.B. Last, 250 E. 64th Street, Chicago, Illinois. On the back of the envelope Baby Doe wrote her comment, "Honeymaid and I opened these letters for the first time Sunday June 28, 1908. Oh my poor broken heart—I must live for Honeymaid's sake. God pity us." What upset Baby Doe was that Lily had married her cousin, John Last. He was ten years older than Lily. His mother was Nealie McCourt Last, a sister to Baby Doe.

*Later November 1980.* — Lily writes how happy she is, and that everything is going very well. She writes about her hsuband Jack: "He is just splendid in every way, and has a disposition much like dear Papa had." She is thinking about Thanksgiving and writes, "We are going to have our Thanksgiving dinner with Claudia and Ralph and Grandma. What fine turkeys you used to cook for us, Mama dear—they were perfection."

In a letter of December 4, 1908, Lily writes that they have a six pound baby girl, and that all is fine. She added that John is a very proud father.

To Lily from Silver about Lily marrying her cousin:

*Our Darling Lily:—*

*We received your letter a couple of days ago and mamma is in bed prostrate with grief because your baby is weaned.*

*She hoped that you would nurse it two years as mamma did us and we never had a sick day except the diptheria and chicken-pox which any baby can catch. Even though you had very little milk for her you should have partly fed her but still nursed her, her second summer may be a very sad thing for you and us all and mamma is wild with grief because you are probably now agin in the family-way and mamma says it will be but a repetition of her martyred Sister Nealia, one child in her womb, one nursing at her breast, one on her lap, one on her dress at her feet, four scarcely able to walk, consequently her blood was impoverished and she went to a premature grave. If Jack is anything like his mother Nealia and we hope he is he will protect you from that if you are not strong enought to protect yourself for she was one of the most beautiful characters ever sent to this world.*

*Dont ever tell any stranger that you have raised your poor little baby scientifically, it only sounds cruel and coarse. Grandma raised fourteen and never lost a baby in her life, raised by pure common sense and love. What do you mean by **science**? Do you mean that you are denying our Lord Jesus Christ and his sufferings. Now that I am also steeped in grief I may as well tell you that I will be very much surprised if you will ever see mamma in this world again for a year ago last May, 1908, she was struck down suddenly in the street one night by a few words said to her with a disease of what is called a dripping heart, her doctor, a very wonderful Swedish doctor says there are only a few cases of it in this world and through Father Guida she is sure of being able to get a Priest when the end comes and the Doctor told me confidentially that there is no hope and that any minute it may all be over. She has taught me to run the mine so I can do as she is doing about every detail. So my prospect of ever crossing the plains again is very slight. I do not like the East but would love to see you all and I am so glad for your lovely invitation to visit you.*

*I have had very flattering offers from all the newspapers and when I will superintend the mine my work in this life will be literary and if I am called to European fields it will be via the Pacific. We would have been independent as I have many manuscripts ready for publication but I hadn't the money for copyrights and dared not trust them unprotected on the market. The mine will be saved, mamma is the most wonderful woman in the world, the most magnificent intelect, fearless and with powerful strength of*

105

*character that she risks all to do the right thing. She is perfectly fearless but alas she is nothing but love Lily, her clinging to the cross and religious life, our Lord Jesus blesses her with visions and interpretations of such. I too have been so blessed through her holy teachings and gentle influences. We are about to close the last deal that will ever be on the Matchless, the attorneys are waiting for her to arise and give the order. She is praying every minute that you will not leave Chicago to make a visit to Green Bay or any small city or anywhere when we are known **until this Matchless deal is closed and at an end** because the newspaper reporters, I am a newspaper woman and I know, will put a piece in the paper about Senator Tabor's daughter marrying her — — — and it will be heralded all over the U.S. and mamma will never rise to dictate and sign the last papers on the Matchless. So I beg you in the name of God my darling Sister to remain in Chicago and let all be quiet and silent. You can not and will not refuse to do this, for my sake. Jack is ten years older than you and he must see the adviseability of the above and take a firm stand and advise you. Nobody in this world but mamma could have ever conquered in this Matchless case and she could and has only through our Lord Jesus Christ. She is so respected, honored and loved by the good citizens of this state for the honorable way in which she has lived that they scream to her acrost streets and stop elevators in midair to wish her God's blessing and success. It is always whenever she is seen in public and in all public places no matter how big they are. It is wonderful.*

*Kiss darling baby for me and know that I love you dearly.*

*Your loving sister Silver*

Baby Doe insisted that Lily and her husband come home at once.

My Own Precious Darling Lily:-

Come home to mamma amd  Honeymaid at once do not delay you and dear Jack

must alwaysalive with us I would never have consented to your being

away but for my poor dear mothers sake I knew you could be a comfort

to her in her last days but npow you are not with her so  I can not have

you away from us I love dear jack derly as I do all of ore darrling

Nealies children and he is good and there is a God my darling child

theree is a  merciful Gopd your telegram or letters were not opened

106

or read until to-day and we did not find your telegram üntil the early
part of thids month as yours and Claudias letters went to Leadville
and back here again and some stayed here so I asked Honeymaid to keep
them all for me so until to-day I only knew what Phil and Wiklard
had said. O my precious darling lily come at pnce and telegraph
me what day you both will be here telegraph me the minute you get this
letter and come at once and never leave us again Lil y darling you
will love Silver she is so dear and it was a crime that you had to be
seperated but she could not go to you it was poverty which is one curse
but we must trust in God come to me my precious darling at once
and you both will be happy and comfortable forever dont fail me come to
us darling Lily you know you were half my poor heart and Honeymaid the
other half come home we love love love you with all our hearts . Forever
  our devotrd and loveing Mamma
Tell John and all the dear Lasts how we suffer for them in their sad
loss and also Jene and all her family How id dear medaline and Dittie.

Lily and her husband never did return to Baby Doe and
Silver. Lily named her oldest child Caroline. In a letter of
1917, Lily mentions another daughter, Jane, who was then six
years old, and Jack, age seven. Lily was a happy and contented
housewife and mother. All through the years she continued to
write affectionate letters to her mother and sister.

Baby Doe and Silver made a few visits to Chicago and
Wisconsin to visit the relatives. Again, in 1917, Lily writes her
mother that "the children talk of you so often. They don't
forget you and often say they wish you would come again."
Caroline and Jane liked the large dolls Baby Doe gave to them.
Lily wrote that Jane was going to look like Baby Doe, and had
such big eyes.

Stories have been circulated about Lily not having anything
to do with her mother or sister. Correspondence proves this to
be untrue.

During all of this Baby Doe and Silver tried to work the
mine, but did not have much luck.

Silver did not have the benefit of tutors as did her sister Lily.
After the loss of the Tabor fortune, Lily and Baby Doe taught
Silver. Mrs. Ryan had been one of the tutors employed by the
Tabors in Denver, who wrote encouraging letters to Silver

wanting her to keep studying and learn all she could without her tutor.

The year 1903 found Silver still writing to Santa Claus and the fairies with long lists of requests. Her letters had been answered in the past. Now she was heart-broken at not having any response to her wants. Finally Silver discovered that her belief in fairies and Santa Claus was all in vain. There were no such things at all. She never would forget the day this truth was made known to her. She felt deceived and broken-hearted, because her belief had been so strong all these years. She lost faith in all around her, and her entire dream world came crashing down at her feet. What a cruel world! This was her greatest disappointment ever. Poor Silver was to experience many more disappointments and failures in future years.

Silver still loved and wanted animals. She had cats all during her lifetime. Baby Doe's brother Pete lived in Denver. Through the years he gave money to Baby Doe and Silver. He bought a pony for Silver, and she learned to ride. She enjoyed riding through the hills and down to Leadville, and was a familiar sight on Leadville streets. The *Herald Democrat* of June 5, 1914 reports a slight accident: "Silver Tabor narrowly escaped serious injury when her saddle pony which she calls Polly slipped on the concrete crossing at 8th and Harrison Avenue, and plunged to the ground. Miss Tabor stayed with the horse and was in the saddle when the animal regained its footing, but she sustained a bad bruise on the knee."

Silver attended school in Leadville and did very well. A friend of Silver's said she was very impressed with Silver's excellent use of English and easy flow of speech despite her speech impediment.

Silver was an unusually bright and intelligent girl. She was happy and jolly and made friends easily. She loved to read and spent hours in the local library, often exchanging books with friends and students.

Silver in later years received letters from many of her old school friends:

*Spokane Wn.*
*Sept. 24, 1911*

*Miss Silver Tabor*
*Matchless Mine*
*Leadville, Colo.*

Dear Friends

*Mrs. & Miss Tabor.:*            *Dear Silver*

*Undoubtedly you will be very much surprised to hear from me, but I still think of you & remember days of school together. I also hope I am not forgotten by you for friendships sake write me a letter.*

*Do you remember Ben Cohn & Bros. of Lead. who were jewelers. They have established here and are a very prominent business concern. I was in & gave them my name & rec'd a glad hand. There I saw your pictures in the window. Why Silver I was so glad to see it. It did look so natural & reminded me of old Lead. Now I'll tell you of my trip since I left. I suppose you have read articles in the newspapers about me. I left Lead. for Denver where I learned dancing & riding. Later accomplished at Salt Lake & left here with Ringling Bros. Played two seasons with them. Just finished an engagement with the Orpheum Circuit. I expect to rest this season & next season I am offered a chance with the Shirly troup. I was married in Omaha, Nebr. May 1, 1907. We are happy & get along fine. I travel by the name of Belle Frye. My old name of Hannah I cast aside. My former name was Hannah Nylander. Now Mrs. B.L. Star. We have a nice home & automobile here. How is everything there. Do you ever see Esther, my sister? They still owe me $125 since I worked for them. I only wish I could collect it. I am coming to Leadville for Xmas. I then see about it. Are they still there in the Dairy business?*

*Now Silver do write me a letter. I am sure it would be the greatest of pleasure to accept it. If you ans. I'll send you one of my pictures in exchange for one of you, if only a postal.*

*How is the "Matchless" coming. Did you keep it? Are you working it?*

*My writting is very poor because I have not fully recovered from my operation of last month. I was in the Sacred Heart Hospital four weeks, was operated on for two abesses in my side. I feel very well now.*

*I wish you could make me a visit with your mother & see sunny old Spokane. We like it fine, better than any other city yet.*

*Please excuse my poor writting as I'll do better next time. Now do ans. soon.*

*With love & kisses I remain as ever a friend, Belle.*

*Mrs. B.L. Starr*
*1406 Olive Ave.*
*Spokane, Wash.*

Spokane Wn
Sept. 24-1911

Miss Silver Tabor.
Matchless Mine
Leadville. Colo.
Dear friends.
Mrs. + Miss Tabor. -: dear Silver
Undoubtedly you
will be very much surprised to
hear from me. but I still think
of you + remember days of school to
gether. I also hope I am not forgotten
by you for friend ships sake write
me a letter.
Do you remember Ben Cohn + Bro
of Lead. who were jewelers. they have
established here. and are a very
Prominent business concern

110

# Chapter Seven
# *Oh, To Be a Writer!*

As Silver grew older, Baby Doe realized the increased responsibility of "bringing up" her daughter. She vowed she would do all possible to protect her little girl from the evils of the world. Silver was an attractive young girl with large soft brown eyes and dark hair. She was about average height, and had a good figure. She spoke in a low pitched and pleasing voice. Her slight lisp added to her charm. She was a romantic girl and was greatly interested in poetry and music. She dreamed of being a writer. She said she would have liked to study dramatic art if she had not had the speech impediment. Silver made early efforts at writing poetry:

### Ode to Claudia

*'Tis only a dream from love's own flame,*
*That mingles in love's sweet sleep,*
*'Tis only a dream from Heaven,*
*That mingles in love so deep,*
*'Tis only a dream of Sweethearts,*
*Who met and were tied with a bow,*
*'Tis only a dream from sunshine,*
*That lights true sweethearts with glow,*
*'Tis only a dream of sunrise,*
*That sweethearts must part.*

### Uncle George's thoughts about Claudia—

*You have no more sympathy for me,*
*Than a cat has for a dog*
*You treat me like a puppy,*
*And set me on a log,*
*You send me to the bog,*
*To dig it out in squares,*
*And I'm haunted,*
*And I'm haunted,*
*By those awful Bancher Bears.*

*Silver Dollar*

1897

111

## YOU'RE TOO YOUNG-MY BOY-MY BOY.
----------------------

Verse No. (I)

Dad has chickens- I won't tell,
Much about 'em but they're swell;
Beauty spots and p'roxide hair,
But I'm telling- that's no fair,
For Dad gives me lots of tin,
Not for whiskey wine or gin,
For he says and makes me mad;
"You're too young-my lad-my lad."
----------------------

Verse No. (2)

Oh, Dad's chickens- they are beaut's,
But those chickens aren't in coops,
For they perch upon his knees,
And the scenery that he sees,
And the lip-stick lips to kiss,
All of this he'd hate to miss,
But my Dad-he says to me;
"You're too young-you see-you see."
----------------------

Chorus.

You're too young-my boy-my boy,
For the chickens, wine and joy,
And the bright lights all aglow,
Where the grownup rounders go,
You run home-my lad-my lad,
Tell your mother that your dad,
Went to lodge to ride the goat,
While I sail away and float,

Seas of booze-ahoy-ahoy,
You're too young-my boy-my boy.

112

FORM

# A

FOR WORKS
MULTIPLIED BY
MECHANICAL
MEANS.

## TITLE.

In the case of a book in more than one volume, a separate title-page for each
volume must be sent.  Only **ONE** copy of each title is required.
The law distinctly specifies a PRINTED title.  If a typewritten title is sent, it is at the claimant's risk.

**No entry can be made on a written title.**

---

**INSERT ON THIS PAGE PRINTED OR TYPEWRITTEN TITLE OR TITLES.**

If several typewritten titles are to be sent with one application, they can be put upon this
page of the application blank, but should be 1 ¼ inches apart, so as to allow the date and number stamp to come between; or they can be on separate sheets of paper.  If necessary,
additional sheets of titles may be inserted between pages 2 and 3, but it is always preferable
to send the regular **printed** title-pages.

THE DARE-DEVIL.          JUN 6 1910

- - - - -

The Dare-devil has come and gone his way,

    With a reckless smile in his eyes of gray,

With curling lips that seem to say;

    I'll turn up again Resurrection Day.

Oh! we've learned a lesson from you- Old Boy;

    Take life as it comes, with it's pain and joy.

- - - - - - - - - - - -

You're a roving sport and you hit the trail,

    In a palace car or beating the rail,

"Till you reach the Port where the great Ships sail;

    And cheer them on with your lusty hail.

As you quaff life's cup you pledge a toast;

    To the Lords and Bums of your loyal host.

- - - - - - - - - - -

With the Belle of the ball- where the lights are low,
   You steal a kiss from her cupid's-bow,
And then the Ranch girl, with her cheeks aglow;
   You kiss in the field where the pumpkins grow.
Which is the sweetest to kiss, of all;
   The naive Ranch girl or the Belle of the ball?

      - - -- - - - - - - - - - -

Ah! life, with it's coffers full of gold,
   That can buy the world, when the price is told,
And life, with it's beggars, young and old;
   Loves a Dare-devil- defiant and bold.
So here's to you. from the bubbles of joy;
   To the dregs of despair- good luck, Old Boy.

      - - - - - - - - - - - - -

114

# HERE'S TO YOU

--------------

### (By- Silver Dollar Tabor)

--------------

Here's to you - you may be sleeping
    In an unmarked grave to-night,
With a wild vine o'er you creeping
    Shyly in the pale starlight.

--------------

Here's to you - a thousand daisies
    May be scattered 'neath your feet,
As your hunted tracks are leading
    To a Vagabonds retreat..

--------------

Here's to you - you may be welcome
    In the ranks of fame and wealth,
Where the kings of power and fortune,
    Are all drinking to your health.

--------------

Here's to you - a haunting memory
    May be calling through the years,
With a pain that joy can't deaden
    And a voice that rings with tears.

--------------

Here's to you - the sun is sinking
    O'er your life - if live you do,
And through all it - are you drinking
    To the one who drinks to you?

115

Years ago a Leadville person gave the author an interesting article written by Mattie Edwards Stuthman, formerly a teacher at Evansville, a district school in Big Evans Gulch. Entitled "High Altitude Memories," it mentioned Silver's life in Leadville: "When I was eight years old, we moved up Big Evans Gulch. Our house was near the Fitzhugh mine, which was at the eastern edge of Fryer Hill, and we were within less than five minutes walk of the famous Matchless Mine. Of course I began to hear a great deal about the Tabors. In all of the years that I heard of Mr. Tabor I never heard him called 'Haw' always H.A.W. Tabor.

"Mrs. Tabor was living at the Matchless. One of our summer trails to town led near the place. Often she was outdoors when we passed. We always waved, Mama would speak to her, but she would just give us a quick nod and hasten indoors.

"One summer day, when I was twelve years old (to the best of my recollection), I decided to ride to my home with the grocery delivery man. Upon arriving at the store, I found that another girl passenger was going to ride too. We clambered up to the high seat of the wagon and off we went.

"I noticed that the girl was about my own age and that she was very attractive, with lovely, large, dark brown eyes. We soon began a conversation and I learned that she was Silver Dollar Tabor. She was spending some time with her mother. I had heard of her and was so glad to see her. Before we came to the place where she had to leave us, we felt as if we had known each other for years and we planned to meet again soon.

"That was the beginning of a short but pleasant friendship. We met frequently and seemed to have so much to talk about. Of course I asked her to come to my home, but Mrs. Tabor didn't wish her to go into our house. We took long walks, exchanged books and discussed them. I called her Silver as she disliked being called Silver Dollar. She had an impediment in her speech. I do not know just what it was. She was not exactly tongue-tied, but there was just a suggestion of that. She said if it weren't for that handicap she would like to study dramatic art.

"Young as I was, I was very much impressed with Silver's excellent English and easy flow of speech despite the impediment. Certainly she was an unusually bright, intelligent girl, always happy and jolly.

"She was obedient to her mother. At first she was not allowed to come into our house, but at the end of that first summer she came, after having coaxed her mother into giving her permission. The following summer she was allowed to have picnic lunches with me.

"Never once did she apologize for her mother in any way, despite Mrs. Tabor's queer way of dressing and the fact that she lived in the old cabin at the Matchless Mine keeping strictly to herself.

"Silver came back to Leadville later summers, but she had changed as she grew older, into somewhat of a harum-scarum sort of person, sometimes dashing around town on horseback. Then she went away for good, but I shall always remember our two summers of delightful friendship."

Many years later Mrs. Stuthman visited Leadville and walked up to the Matchless Mine. "We knocked on Mrs. Tabor's door, but although we could hear her move a chair and rattle a stove lid, she did not answer. I called to her, 'I am an old friend of Silver Dollar,' but no response."

This article was later published in Colorado Magazine of 1952.

Silver Dollar was obedient as a young girl and her mother kept trying in every way to keep her from wrong doing and evil ways.

As she grew older, Silver felt she must start gaining experience for her writing career. Almost daily, Silver would go to the *Herald Democrat* newspaper office seeking a job as reporter. She spent time there without pay, writing articles. The editor, H.C. Butler, admired her beauty, but did not think she had talent worthy of hire. Although she could not get work there, Silver did not give up, and was pleased that Mr. Butler did loan her a typewriter. She "pecked away" trying to learn to type. She typed her poetry and stories she had already written. At one time she had a trunk filled with manuscripts.

The author always enjoyed talking to a very dear friend, Mrs. Theresa O'Brien. She lived on West Seventh Street when I knew her. As a young girl, her family lived at Evansville, a small settlement just east of Leadville. There were the usual stores and saloons. Mrs. O'Brien remembered Silver Dollar Tabor when they were young school girls. She said, "I sometimes went with a friend Hazel Gorris and Silver Dollar to the Opera House Barns to get horses to ride." This livery and feed stable was located in back of the Opera House on St. Louis Avenue. It is interesting to note that many years before this, as seen in the Leadville directory of 1887, this business was owned by the Younger Brothers, notorious outlaws of the time. Later they moved their business to S. Pine Street. Mrs. O'Brien continued, "The owner of the Opera House Barns that was there when we were young kept very fine horses. He always gave the best horse to Silver Dollar. It was a palomino with a yellow bridle. Hazel and I were given just any old horse. I remember how put out we were about this, and we never did forget it." In later years this man at the barns was reported to be the one that led Silver Dollar astray and seduced her.

Mr. and Mrs. Walter Peck were old time residents of Leadville. They lived for years on East Tenth Street. Interesting and likeable people, the author enjoyed visiting with them. They remembered Silver Dollar and her mother when they lived in the two hundred block on East Tenth Street, a house since torn down. Mr. Peck said, "I remember Silver Dollar had a very close friend named Katherine Fitzgerald, also living near the Tabors on the same street and block. They were both beautiful girls—Silver Dollar with large brown eyes and dark hair and the other girl had taffy colored hair and big brown eyes." The Pecks remembered how well dressed both girls were: "They wore beautiful dresses and had beautiful horses. They rode side saddle, and we often saw them riding by our house."

The author asked Mr. Peck, "What ever happened to the Fitzgerald girl?" Mr. Peck replied, "Oh, she met a salesman that came here to Leadville. He sold silk. She ended up going to Denver with him, and later to China. She didn't marry him, just lived with him."

* * * * *

Theodore Roosevelt came to Colorado on a bear hunt. There was great excitement when he came to Leadville. Silver pushed through the crowds to see him, and was thrilled by his visit. She was so inspired that she later wrote the lyrics to a song for him entitled, "Our President Roosevelt's Colorado Hunt." On the center cover was a fine picture of Teddy Roosevelt. To the left were the words: "March Song." Below that: "To the memory of the late U.S. Senator H.A.W. Tabor, and music by Professor A.S. Lohman." To the right of the picture: "Words by Silver Echo Tabor, Dedicated to my Beloved Father H.A.W. Tabor." At the bottom of the picture: "Published by Silver Echo Tabor. Author of 'Spirits,' 'Love and Lilies,' and 'In a Dream I Loved You,' Denver, Colorado."

Baby Doe saved enough money to have it published in 1908. The Tabor family was very proud of Silver's accomplishment. the Denver *Post* of August 9, 1908, carried an article and account of her talent. Silver's picture, used with the article, and her name in headlines was great encouragement to her.

Two years later while Silver was employed in Denver, working in a newspaper office, she met Teddy Roosevelt again on another of his Colorado visits. He gave an address in Denver. This time she was introduced to him as the author of his song, a musical tribute to the famous Teddy Roosevelt. The Denver "Press Club—Chuck Wagon Eat" at Overland Park was enjoyed by Teddy where he ate cowboy style. He loved the West and the great outdoors of Colorado. Roosevelt posed for a picture with Silver and he thanked her for the song. Denver newspapers printed the picture showing him shaking hands with Silver. Again the Tabor family and friends were delighted.

January 30, 1908 Silver typed a letter to President Roosevelt informing him of the song she had written for him.

Leadville, Colo. Jan. 30, 1908.

President Theodore Roosevelt

The White House, Washington, D. C.

My Dear MR. President:-

I enclose a song about your Colorado hunt of which I am the Author.

I have sent a copy of it to the leader of your Band,
desireing him to assist me in having grand Military music put
to it so that the Bands in greeting you , dear President might
honor me by playing it.

I sincerely hope it will please you as it is my most
earnest desire to have it do so.

My father was a most ardent admirer of you as is the whole
World and were he alive, no thing would make him so happy as
to have his daughter have the high honor of pleasing you

I have the honor to remain most respectfully yours.

Silver    Tabor.

Copy.

Judge Lindsey sends Silver a letter of thanks for the copy of
her song. He gives her encouragement.

JUDGE's CHAMBERS
County Court
Juvenile Court
DENVER, COLO.
BEN B. LINDSEY, JUDGE

September 25, 1908.

Miss Silver Tabor,

C/o Mrs.H.A.W.Tabor,

Leadville, Colorado.

My dear Silver:

I do not believe that I have acknowledged your
kindness in sending me the copy of your song entitled, "Our
President Roosevelt's Colorado Hunt." I got home the first
of the month and found a large mass of correspondence, and
it was only because of this fact that the song did not
reach me until only recently.  I want you to know it was
not for lack of appreciation that this tardy reply is made,

and I wish to apologize to you for it and trust you will accept
the explanation offered.

Now, my dear little girl, you do not know how much
I appreciate your thoughtfulness and kindness, and I want
you and your good mother to know that anything I can do to
be of service to you I will consider it a special privilege
and pleasure. I want to tell you that I was really surprised
at the excellence of your words and the beautiful sentiment
of your song. I am sure that you have talent in this direction, and you must feel encouraged to develop it, even though
your first work should not meet with the success it deserves,
which is generally the case with all new writers, but I should
think that your song would have a wide sale. It certainly deserves it.

I wish you every success.

With kindest regards and best wishes, I am,

Sincerely your friend,

A letter to Mrs. Graves from Silver refusing to change
words or music to her song.

Leadville, Colo. July 7, 1910?

Mrs. Nellie Davenport Graves,

Denver, Colo.

My Dear Mrs. Graves:-

I have not received your letter addressed to Cherokee
St. and we thank you very much for your kind thoughts and wishes.

Under no conditions would I or mamma permit the music
on words of my song, "Our President Roosevelt's Colorado Hunt"
changed or used in any way. We consider Prof. Lohman's music to

121

perfeetly beautiful and were we not equally pleased with the words
we never would havš gone to the expenoe of publishing it.

We dšarly love Prof. Lohman and to us the song is perfeet.

Be were so sorry not to have had the pleasure of
saying good-bye to you and Mrs and Mrs. Earlenbaoh and we sineerely
hope for your suooess in all your undertakings. Plsasš give
our love to them. It will give us great pleasure to eall aned
see you all ås soon as we return. The light on this maohine is
poor so I ean't do a very good job.

   With llove from mamma ,

     Your loving.

      Silver.

Another selected letter of congratulations from Silver's
sister Lily.

> *My Darling,*
> *I can't tell you how happy you made us with your*
> *beautiful song. It is just grand and I am so, so proud of you,*
> *my dear dear sister. It cannot help but make a great success*
> *and you must keep right on with the fine work. I cannot*
> *realize you really did it—it seems too wonderful. Your*
> *picture is lovely and I wish you would send me one so we*
> *can always have it before us on the wall. The firelight on*
> *Pres. Roosevelts face is so effective and the music is*
> *splendid too.*
> *Pres. Roosevelt must have been complimented and this is*
> *just the right time for this to come out.*
> *Jack was so glad to get his copy too—and took it down*
> *town with him and showed it to everyone at the office.*
> *We were glad too to get the newspaper clippings. You are*
> *certainly a wonder Mamma dear, and you have made a*
> *great fight.*
> *Will write soon again and write to us often. With love*
> *and a big hug for the composer of "Pres. Roosevelt's 'Bear*
> *Hunt'."*
>      *Lovingly, Lily*

Silver needed encouragement, and should have kept up her
work until she reached her dream of success. She also lacked
the money to have other works published and promoted.

Thanks to her mother, the Roosevelt song was published. Somehow Baby Doe managed to scrape up enough money to publish it. Her song failed to receive great success, but she was not completely discouraged—she would try again.

Silver loved the West, and read many western novels. Her research for a book she hoped to write prompted her to write to Buffalo Bill—W.F. Cody. She asked him to tell her of his Buffalo hunts and fights with the Indians. She received a very nice answer, and Mr. Cody had great praise for her father, H.A.W. Tabor:

> *The New HOFFMAN HOUSE*
> *Madison Square*
> *New York, Feb. 10, 1908*
>
> *Dear Silver,*
>
> *Of course I will tell you of some of my Buffalo hunts and fights with the Indians. But I never killed either without feelings of regret and remorse. But then some one had to do it. Some one had to stand between civilization and savagery. Someone had to make it possible for civilization to advance.*
>
> *I loved and respected your noble Father who done so much for Denver. It's the pioneer who opens up the way and makes it easy for those who follow. Risks his life and fortune and is soon forgotten. Your dear Father was one. And your Mother. She is the best woman Colorado has ever known. How I would like to meet you both. Please let her know that I have often thought of her.*
>
> *I hope you are both well and happy. I am just leaving for Washington. I will be home at Cody, Wyo. during the month of March. From there I will send you the stories. Please write again for I love you all.*
>
> *God bless you*
> *W.F. Cody*

OUR PRESIDENT ROOSEVELT'S COLORADO HUNT

MARCH SONG.

PRICE 50¢

TO THE MEMORY OF THE LATE U.S. SENATOR H.A.W. TABOR

WORDS BY SILVER ECHO TABOR

DEDICATED TO MY BELOVED FATHER H.A.W. TABOR

MUSIC BY PROF. A.S. LOHMANN

PUBLISHED BY SILVER ECHO TABOR
AUTHOR OF "SPIRITS" "LOVE AND LILIES" AND "IN A DREAM I LOVED YOU."
DENVER, COLO.

# OUR PRESIDENT ROOSEVELT'S COLORADO HUNT

Words by SILVER ECHO TABOR

Music by A.S. LOHMANN

Roll up in a Na - va - jo
Way up on the crest - ed
Passed by the bit - ing

blan - ket And stretch 'neath the sweet pine trees, With the
sum - mits, I'll brave the fran - tic storm, And
winds, Still in the beam - ing sun,

125

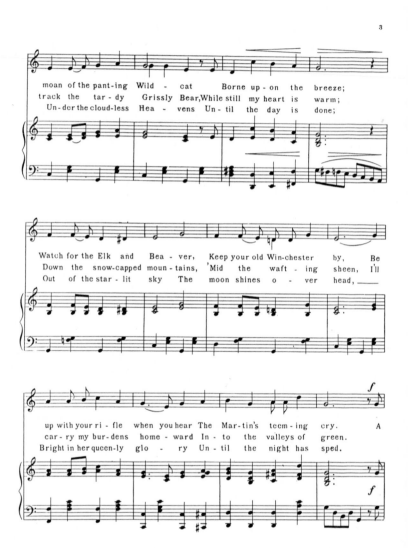

moan of the pant-ing Wild - cat    Borne up - on the    breeze;
track the   tar - dy   Grissly Bear,While still   my heart is     warm;
Un - der the cloud-less Hea - vens Un - til   the day is      done;

Watch for the Elk   and    Bea - ver,   Keep your old Win-chester    by,    Be
Down the snow-capped moun-tains, 'Mid the    waft - ing   sheen,  I'll
Out  of the star - lit   sky  The   moon shines  o  -  ver    head,____

up with your ri - fle    when you hear The  Mar-tin's  teem - ing    cry.    A
car - ry my bur - dens  home - ward In - to   the   valleys of    green.
Bright in her queen-ly  glo  -  ry  Un - til   the   night has    sped.

way, a - way, to the glo-ri-ous wilds, Where life is free and the
Dream, ah! dream, of the life with-in the hills, And peace-ful slumber by the
Live, oh! live, 'neath the az - ure Heaven, Un - til the gold - en

world your own, Up - on the slopes 'mid the shel - t'ring pines, And
rip - pling rills Up - on the slopes 'mid the wind - swept pines That
morn is giv'n, Out to the land of free - dom, Sweet

*ril.* *a tempo*

down in the val - leys I'll roam, Wrapped in a
stand like Sen - ti - nels round, Wrapped in a
with the scent - ed breeze, Wrapped in a

Na - va - jo blan-ket, I'll make the West my home.
Na - va - jo blan-ket, I'll keep watch with my hound.
Na - va - jo blan-ket, I'll pal with the old pine trees.

127

CHORUS

Wrapped in a Na-va-jo blan-ket In the land of bliss,

Blaz-ing the dar-ing hun-ter's trail, Free in the wil-der-ness; The

bu-gle call of the wild, wild West Is the Coyote's cry in the hour of rest,

Warm in my Na-va-jo blan-ket, I'll live life at its best.

Denver Public Library Western Collection

**Silver Dollar Tabor meets President Roosevelt at a press club dinner, August 29, 1910.**

THE NEW
HOFFMAN HOUSE,
MADISON SQUARE,
J. P. CADDAGAN. Manager.

NEW YORK, *Feb. 10* 1908

ABSOLUTELY FIRE PROOF.

My Dear Silver.
Of course
I will tell you of some
of my Buffalo hunts and
fights with the Indians. But
I never killed either without
feelings of regret and
remorse. But there some
one had to do it. Some
one had to stand between
civilization and savagery.
Some one had to make it
possible for civilization
to advance. I loved and
respected your noble father
who done so much for
Denver. He the pioneer who
opens up the way. And makes

130

it easy for those who follow. Risks his life and fortune. And is so soon forgotten. Your dear Father was one. And Your Mother. She is the best woman Colorado has ever known. How I would like to meet you both. Please let her know that I have often thought of her. I hope you are both well and happy. I am just leaving for Washington. I will be home at Cody. Wyo. during the Month of March. from there I will send you the stories. Please write again. for I love you all.

God bless you

W. F. Cody

All during her lifetime Silver had difficulty with not being able to keep her trunks. Often they were sold for charges. She writes of her problems.

Denver, Colorado, April 1st, 1909.

Mr.A.D.Parker,

     Denver, Colorado.

Dear Sir:

     I checked a trunk from Leadville to Denver last August. The check No. was 84121. It came by the Colorado Midland, and C. & S. I presented the check and applied for the trunk many times, also my mother and friends applied and they failed to locate it. The 18th of March, 1909, I applied again at the Union Depot with my check, and they promised again to look it up, and told me they had moved it to the C. & S. Warehouse. About the 21st of March upon making application again I was informed that the C. & S. had sold it for $3.50 March 3rd, although my name in full was all through it, and we carefully examined the record of said sale and found out that there was no record of who it was sold to. I have the check of that trunk in my possession. The actual loss to me is not less than $7,500.00, and I think much more. In that trunk there were manuscripts that I have no copy of, which are lost to me forever by the above named sale. Please authorize settlement at once of said claim, for if you fail to, I must at once sue the C. & S., and I positively have evidence that will compel the C. & S. to pay my claim.

     Yours very truly,

*Silver Echo Tabor*
*Genl. Delve. City.*

(In duplicate.)

132

THE COLORADO & SOUTHERN RAILWAY COMPANY
DENVER, COLO.

T. E. FISHER
GENERAL PASSENGER AGENT

April 8, 1909.

Miss Silver Echo Tabor,

General Delivery,

Denver, Colo.

Dear Miss:--

Your communication of the 1st
addressed to Mr. Parker, Vice-President, of
this Company, in reference to trunk which you
checked from Leadville to Denver has been
referred to me for reply.

As our General Baggage Agent advised
you in person some days ago, this trunk was
sold at public auction, together with a lot of
other baggage to pay storage charges.

The record of the Denver Union Depot
baggage room was that no call was made for this
baggage up to the time same was advertised for
sale.

The baggage in question was received
at the Denver Union Depot August 21, 1908, and
was placed in the loft with other unclaimed
baggage September 22nd, and taken thence to
our storage room Oct. 21st and was sold on
March 3rd.

Under the law it is only necessary
for us to hold the baggage 90 days; however,
this baggage was held 194 days.

Your claim is respectfully declined.

Yours truly,

F

Silver's continued interest in animals is shown by another
letter of January 16, 1911, a reply to her inquiry about
obtaining a baby wildcat.

*PRISCILLA RANCH*
*Gleneyre, Colo., Jan. 16, 1911*
*Miss S.D. Tabor—Denver, Colo.*
    *Your letter of inquiry of recent date relative to baby wild-
cat received and contents noted. In reply I would say that in
the Spring I will try and locate a den of kittens and if
successful will advise you.*
                    *Yours very truly,*
                    *A. DeV Baldwin*

Silver still felt she must get experience working in
newspaper offices. This she believed would insure her future
as a successful writer.

Her Uncle Peter McCourt continued to supply her with
some money until she could support herself. In Denver Silver
finally did get on the staff of the Denver *Times.* She managed
to rent a small, cheap room near the Windsor Hotel and was
somewhat encouraged when a few of her stories were accepted
and published by Denver newspapers.

Silver had written a friend of hers in Watkins, Colorado,
giving her advice about marriage. Her friend, Agnes,
responds:

                    *Watkins, Colo.*
                    *Dec. 15, '11*
*Dear Silver:*
    *I received your two letters and in the first I was quite
alarmed when I heard how the operation on your nose
affected you but if it was successful you will feel so much
better now.*
    *I am coming into Denver Sunday and I am glad. I love
the country but it gets so tiresome. I have a nice cowboy out
here but I am not going to marry him or anybody else for a
long time to come. It feels too good to be free and know that
you are not married, to go and tie up now would be a
catastrophe so I am keeping out of that.*
    *I'll not show him the letters nor anybody else. I know
perfectly well that anything you said to me was said for my
own good and I took it in the spirit in which it was meant.
So don't you worry and I don't like you less, I like you more
because of the interest you took in me. Everything you said
was perfectly true and it was kind of you to write such a
letter to a friend for fear they might become fractious and go*

A. DeV. BALDWIN

CATTLE
HORSES

PRISCILLA RANCH

Glenespie, Colo., Jan. 16th 1911

Miss S. D. Tabor
Denver. Colo.

Your letter of inquiry of recent date, relative to baby wild-cat recd and contents noted. In reply I would say that in the Spring I will try and locate a den of kittens, and if successful, will advise you.

Yours very truly,
A. deV. Baldwin

135

*and marry a fellow they didn't know whether they cared for or not.*

*Well I am coming in Denver and I will let you know where I am staying and if you could get up and see me I'd be so glad. I'd like you to come Monday or Tuesday if you could. Hoping you are well and happy, I remain,*

*Your loving friend,*
*Agnes*

A newspaper article, "In the Streets of all Nations" by Silver Dollar Tabor mentions some of the elite of Denver—"The haughty thirty six"—taking part in a fund raising event for charity. It all took place on a Denver main street. Various items were sold in beautifully decorated booths. Those taking part in the event were cleverly dressed to represent people of various countries, etc. Silver's article is as follows:

### IN THE STREETS OF ALL NATIONS

By Silver Dollar Tabor

Saturday

The curtain has fallen over a panorama which will make the dream of a day nursery and settlement house a reality. The haughty thirty-six clasped hands with efficacious society and they labored side by side for sweet chanty's sake. A great heap of money was left behind, the gold of the rich and the silver and copper of the poor.

Thursday night

The first vision that made you wonder if you had been doped, made you think you were seeing things, etc. was Virginia Case as a milkmaid. Well the men didn't go any further, they thought they had their moneys worth and were afraid that things would get more daring and they'd lose their breath entirely.

Christopher Field Clay to wit won a red and yellow jockey cap and indulged in his legal oratory to sell a Steinway Grand piano. Mrs. Clay took the part of an unsophisticated counting girl. Who was the big yellow Teddy bear that was followed everywhere by a crowd? It was Jo Langer, popular newspaper man and "Champion photographer of the world," so Batting Nelson says. Bat knows. Miss Rathoon hovered like a tantalizing illusion behind a tarlatan curtain, she was a turkish pipe dream that made you want more pipe. Margaret Evans was

136

beautiful as a Colonial girl and admirers gave her coins not for a program, but for a smile.

Mrs. Willis Victor Elliot and Mrs. Oscar Malo took a leading part and worked like a dray team. Their efforts were liberally rewarded for their charitable energy was recognized and imparted to others. They had charge of the Street of old Ireland where their artistic originality was displayed. Willis Elliot was on the job too and made the race track as successful as his race for office. Everyone was just as eager to bet for his return in the race as they were to cast their vote for him. Miss Madeline Wilkins, a striking blonde, and Miss Edna Monnigan were wonderful workers and sold so many tickets to the Irish Theatre which was continually crowded when the main attraction was a graceful dance by Miss Lowry Parker.

Tom O'Donnell was captured by a group of barbarous Spanish senoritas who played ring around a rosy and took him down the main street. He couldn't get away and the imposing Thomas looked concerned.

Virginia Page spilled chocolate on her white stocking and then tried to paint it over with white paint which made it look worse.

Ruby Burkhart was a sparkling Dutch beauty and sang a love song to the blushing Theodore Kostitch. The next fellow she sang to was Harold Stephen who was likewise confused but went home cherishing the vision of the laughing, tantalizing little beauty.

Miss Persis Tabor, fresh and girlish was the real Queen of Hearts in the French Cafe. She collected both hearts and money in great quantities, for who wouldn't buy dizzy drinks from such a fascinating waitress.

The harem was weird and dim and redolent with mystery fascinating social leaders lured the men of their set behind the screens where all they did to them was make them smoke and drink coffee supposed to be unadulterated with tingling things and flirt with them through veils. The fortune telling tent was well patronized by all classes including a doctor whose name was with those wanting to know about a certain grass-widow whose name is Genevieve.

A certain young Texan, by name of Jack who wanted to know how long he could be friendly with Genevieve without being sued for breach of promise and Genevieve herself wanted to know if she would ever pull hair again

137

with one of her rivals. All this and lots more went on in the secret den of the fortune teller.

Mrs. Bartelds was a Harem woman in gorgeous blue and sold candy. The men who ridicule candy bought and ate it anyway—just because? Bob Davis, a very prominent local Elk proudly waved a purple and white pennant and was one of the "good fellows" of the Elk night.

The last performance in the Holland Theatre was when Mr. Francis played old scotch airs, "Wash them knees" and Ben Bates when he appeared. They had that special Scotch feature because it was Caledonian night.

Saturday night

The beauty and the beast of Saturday night was Miss Adell Probst and Ted Simans who looked like the latest brand of fake Indian with war paint in evidence. He led Miss Probst around shouting, "Take a chance on Salomie, maybe you get her if you win", and such a Salomie such a siren in a sea green robe with burnished hair. Who wouldn't take a chance but Ted Simans wasn't taking any chances by letting anyone else have them. Miss Probst was the sleeping beauty in the Oriental Theatre in the afternoon and she surely was born for that part. Miss Corinne Johnson was a bewitching Dutch girl in the Windmill dance. Her glorious titian hair looked too beautiful to be real. The great braids really "growed" when on most of the other girls they were just pinned. Ben Bates sang and was encored and then gave right of way to Marguerite Bates who had a group of youthful admirers in knee britches on the other side of the footlights. Jo Langer was auctioneer, he sold dollies for big prices and turned the doll booth into a mint. They bought because Jo offered. He made three dollar dolls look worth twenty-five. It was a fashionable crowd he sold to. Mayor Speer is proud today for the benefit of which he was such a powerful factor was a success.

Author's note: Persis Augusta Tabor was the daughter of Maxcy Tabor. She married a dashing young Frenchman, Paul Alien La Forgue on February 24, 1914.

Silver worked for a time in Denver and also was employed for a short period by the Pueblo, Colorado *Chieftain*. When her editor indicated she was not showing enough progress she quit and started her own little newspaper called *Silver Dollar Weekly*. Eventually she ran out of funds and the enterprise nded. Another disappointment. Would her bad luck ever change?

She did have many fans and admirers, as this sampling of etters indicates:

*THE ROBSON HOUSE*
                        *St. James, Mo., 1-19-1910*
*Miss Silver Dollar Echo Tabor, Denver Colo.*
*My dear Miss Tabor*
    *Being very much impressed with a photo of yours in a St. Louis paper & very anxious to know you better am taking the liberty to write & ask for at least one reply from you. This being a very small favor at the same time means a great deal more to me. Do hope you will see your way clear to at least let me explain myself to you.*
    *My address for the next wk. or ten days will be Marquette Hotel, St. Louis, Mo. Trusting that you will not take offense at this & will look at it in the same light as I do.*
    *I am always,*
                        *Your friend*
                        *F.E. Bodt*


                        *Alton, Ill.*
                        *Jan. 10, 1910*
*Miss Silver Dollar Echo Tabor*
    *I am very sorry to here that your Father has lost his fortune and I am more sorry for you. You must have had an awfully sad Birthday I am sorry to here but Miss Silver Dollar I am writing you these few lines to ask you if you could come to Illinois to my City. I would like to have you in my studio to write storys and music. I am an artist and if you came to my City I will sertenly take good care of you and will make you a nice house and will make every thing pleasent for you. Please send me one of your pictures and write and let me know if you will come to Illinois.*
                        *Most respectfully*
                        *Yours, Harry M. Hamilton*
                        *329 Belle st.*
                        *Alton, Ill.*


                        *Pryor, Okla., Sept. 15. '11*
*Miss Silver Dollar Tabor,*
*c/o Denver Post, Denver, Colo.*
*My dear Miss Tabor,—*

When Silver Dollar's photo appeared in newspapers, it prompted many letters from ardent male admirers.

## The Robson House

St. James, Mo., 1-19 19 10

Miss Silver Dollar Echo Tabor
Denver Colo

My Dear Miss Tabor

Being very much impressed
with a photo of yours in a
St Louis paper & very
anxious to know you
better am taking the
liberty to write & ask
for at least one reply
from you, This being
a very small favor at the
same time means a great
deal more to me. do
hope you will see your

Your poem, "The Dare-Devil" in the Post's Magazine Section of July 23 caught my eye.

How would you like to correspond with an Oklahoma ex-cowboy that is also interested in the fields of composition work?

I am enclosing my first attempt, "The Cowboy." I also write short stories but I believe I am best at humorous work.

Your composition show originality and it expresses something. So many of the poems of today—there is nothing to them.

Gee, how I'd like to be up at Glenwood Springs, Colo. now! It has been the hottest here this summer ever known. The past week has been the most sultry of the summer.

The three summers previous to this one I spent in California. Hence the intense heat was more severe on me than if I had been here all the time.

The Royal Gorge and the Grand Canon are the most beautiful scenery I have ever scene.

For fear this isn't interesting to you will close with the hopes that I may have the pleasure of hearing from you soon.

Yours Resptly;
E.A Shirley

(Typewritten copy of poem enclosed with his letter)

142

## Chapter Eight
# *The Star of Blood*

Silver somehow saved $100 and was anxious to write her long dreamed of novel. She felt she could do better in Chicago, so off she went to write her book. It was a novel of crime entitled *Star of Blood.* She lived in cheap rooming houses and hotels. Determined to make a success of this novel, she worked diligently long hours at a time.

It was the story of Allen Hench Downen, a notorious outlaw of the West. His life of crime started at the age of twelve and continued throughout the book. His sweetheart, and the heroine, was Artie Dallas.

The book itself was a stiff paperback, grey in color with bold red lettering. The grey was chosen purposely to represent the precious metal, silver that had brought the Tabor fortune. Under the title is a large red star, and the name of the author, Silver Dollar Tabor, appears at the bottom of the cover.

Artie Dallas was obviously patterned after Silver herself. A photograph of Allen Downen appears in the book, as well as an illustration of Artie drawn by Silver which strongly resembles Silver. A drawing of Rosie Olson reveals some of Silver's artistic talents.

Although the book is extremely rare, the author was able to locate a copy of it in a Denver rare book store and the entire volume is reproduced here:

**Silver Dollar Tabor—the authoress.**

# Star of Blood

*By* SILVER DOLLAR TABOR

# Star *of* Blood

---

The final chapter is not finished. Perhaps it has not yet begun in the eventful life of the most daring, heartless yet resoluble desperado that ever struck the hidden vein of terror in the bold heart of the heroic West.

Death reigned as monarch where'er his wild trail led, and despair, like a warning spectre followed in his wake. His path through life leads to and fro across our plains and towering mountains with blood marking the way and the memory of his crimes, like vengeful phantoms, perpetually haunting his tracks.

The stepping-stones which have led him to the cell at Canon City are the grave-stones of the fellow beings he murdered and his own gravestone will be a stepping-stone into the great beyond where his natural honor will turn the tables on his crime.

Brigandage and wholesale slaughter were the cards he nonchalantly played in his game of life. The game is not yet finished, still another round will be dealt by the master hand of human fate before the winner is at last proclaimed, before the life of Allen Hence Downen is the dower of the law or again won in freedom by himself.

Who can at this time judge? None can foretell the winner, that secret is hidden in the unread pages of the future and destiny will be the single voter in the campaign of Number 4178.

Solemn juries have justly pronounced verdicts of guilty, his name has branded the history of the Occident with the blood of his victims, and the pall of mourning has been eternally lowered over festal scenes and innumerable lives by the snap of the trigger, by the flash and report of his weapon, but more vitally by the cruelty that controlled the throbbing of his heart.

Allen Hence Downen is a character in late history and present interest that has no rival. The championship for the honors of carnage is his, undisputed.

Within the grim walls of the penitentiary at Canon City, Colorado, is the bandit whose power in "sticking people up" was his dauntless bravado, whose power with himself was his dominant courage but more especially his self-confidence.

He was his own pal and own accomplice, concentrated within this one man was a band of imaginary highwaymen, who, although they were not realities were at least very effective in the robberies that the lone freebooter accomplished.

Like a gentleman of leisure he is incarcerated behind the relentless bars of a prison where his innate elegance of manner is a rare example for his comrades, and the sentence is for life and will be for life if the law has its way, but heretofore with all its power it seldom has at the hands of this prisoner.

Only retrospection alters the sullen fire of his eyes, only one memory draws a tender tear to the stormy surface and that is the memory of his love for a woman of the Bowery whose cadaver is buried in the Potter's field.

He is now sixty years old, his mocking gray eyes are piercing and his dare-devil glance is sure and steady. His cynical features betray a nature; sullen under compulsion and bright under tenderness. His perfect ear is a single mark of his better-self while his receding forehead and upper lip denote an absorbing hunger for love and consideration. The lines that mutely speak of the peril of his conquests are long and drawn. From under his sunken eyes protrudes a nose that is obdurate and prominent and his vicious-looking teeth are filled full of yellow gold. His thin sandy hair grows far back from his oblique brow, his fair mustache hangs straight downward at the ends and he is gaunt and stoop-shouldered.

In 1851 he was born in Polk County, Missouri. His father was the most respected and able attorney of the county, a high-stepping, high-bred gentleman with a tinge of Southern chivalry in his manner. He owned one of the grandest homes in the state. His mother was a social leader and kept open house to all the distinguished people who came that way and the history of the old estate still rings with the romance and gayety of the days of Judge Downen's prosperity.

When the war broke out one of his brothers joined the North and another the South; the "boy in blue" came home or to what was left of the home, for the war had swept away their wealth.

Little did his parents apprehend that the innocent, helpless offspring whose unfortunate birth they were responsible for would become the most famous bandit of the frontier, that he would mature into the wildest, most complete example of barbarism that has ever had the victorious opportunity of baffling the police of a civilized age.

Yet to this fate he was born and the guiding star of his life was one of murder. His initial years were spent innocently where he was born, but at the age of twelve, in 1863, he came to Colorado with his parents, three brothers and two sisters. His latent instincts had not yet betrayed themselves, but an undercurrent, it matters not how deep it runs, will, in the course of time as fate revolves the wheel flow into view, and in 1873 he committed his first crime by murdering a farmer by the name of Townsend and stealing a mule from a brother of County Commissioner Twombly.

This tragedy occurred on a drowsy autumn afternoon; Townsend and Downen were working on a ranch just out of Denver, they were in a mesa where the ripening harvest glowed in the light of the sunset like a realized Eldorado and the lazy river hummed as it tumbled over its sandy bed.

The quarrel started over the possession of Twombly's mule and on the spur of his awakening impulse, Downen brutally murdered his companion with a blunt farm instrument.

He then rapaciously appropriated the beast and in his boyish manner did not even suspect or accuse himself of murder or robbery, but he was arrested and pleaded that he had murdered Townsend in self-defense. He was bailed out of the bull-pen with a four hundred dollar bond, which was signed by David Downen and Philip Ireland. The presiding District Attorney was M.

A. Rogers and David C. Wyatt could boast of the soothing sensations connected with the office of sheriff.

Downen then skipped westward across the fortress of the Rocky Mountains to California and the bond was ungraciously forfeited.

In fresh fields the fugitive found fresh clover and like a bull-calf plunged headlong into the rampant melee of frontier life. It was all new to him and as maddening as a scarlet banner to his teeming youth, whose frenzy lay hidden in the cool steady glance of the searching gray eyes.

He opened his performance in that district with his famous single-handed stage robbery. He was at that time twenty-two and obtained work in a sawmill near Visalia in Tulare County, under the auspicious guise of an ignorant boy from out a sleepy Missouri village, where their only accomplishments are baking corn-bread and cussing in a gentle mile-long drawl. After awhile he became intimately acquainted with the lonely Wells-Fargo agent who took comfort in his comradeship, and one day through his keen strategy he learned that a neat little pile of six thousand dollars was to be sent away on the stage the next night. When the sun sank into the green depths of the restless ocean the following evening he was well armed, and cautiously selecting the most favorable location for a lone boy highwayman to intimidate a whole stage full of red-blooded westerners, with, perhaps a single, unprotected tenderfoot thrown in for luck, but for some unaccountable reason the driver changed his route and Downen's plans were frustrated.

He thus failed to get the plunder he had depended upon, the disappointment only aggravated his anger and his second attempt, which occurred the next night, proved more successful.

He met the stage on the most obscure portion of the road near San Francisco, where he felt safe from impertinent interruption. His boyish figure was held up proudly by the importance of his charge and his face was hidden under a black mask.

"Hands up, if you please, ladies and gentlemen, and be d—— quick about it," his slurring southern voice rang out insolently.

"Keep 'em all well covered pals," was his next order, given to a virtual band of confederates, presumably in ambush on either side of the narrow road.

The driver gazed cross-eyed into the threatening barrels of two large bulldogs and it was hands up for sure and without protest. Downen then very quietly and graciously ordered the occupants of the stage "down and out" and with profound ceremony relieved the travelers and treasure box of five hundred and eighty-five dollars. He then loaded them all back into their respective seats, headed the fractious horses on their way, wished them good luck in a hearty western fashion, and bidding a polite bood-bye, made his escape.

Vest Towers, the driver, drove his foaming horses into San Francisco and excitedly reported that a band of at least a dozen robbers had held them up, when Downen, in reality, had done the job alone.

Tulare County was indignant at the nerve displayed at the hold-up and the gallant men who gloried in daring venture formed posses, and scattering in all directions, dug up the country in a mad effort to capture the whole band of robbers who had just initiated themselves into the fraternity of "Hard Luck," but the game kid bandit was too cute to submit to being lynched and laid low during the hottest part of the hunt.

In a few days the novelty wore off the baffling situation and the bold frontiersmen turned in at their bunk houses.

With proud satisfaction and his little bunch

Silver Dollar Tabor

ARTIE DALLAS

of booty Downen boarded a train for San Francisco and visited during the journey with the husky sheriff of Tulare County, who happened to be on the same train after a vain search for the stage-robbers. As they sat together in the smoking-car Downen's pockets were loaded with a mask, the revolvers that had faced the music, the jewelry he had collected from the travelers and the five hundred and eighty-five dollars. Very freely he talked to the sheriff about the robbery and expressed apparently genuine sympathy for the victims.

Don Vasquez, the Mexican bandit, who was a California stage-robber of enviable renown, was accused of this robbery, but for lack of evidence was released.

From San Francisco Downen went to Denver and St. Louis, but the rich opportunities open in California had a magnetic charm for him and he returned in six months and for the second time, unaided and alone, he held up the same stage line. Vest Towers looked nervously into the two enormous revolvers again, the same supple boyish figure had halted the rearing teams and the same sweetly slurring voice coolly gave orders which were unanimously obeyed. After trimming the whole bunch for all they could boast of the

masked figure gracefully did the honors of brigandage, but hesitated long enough to raise his
mask a little and sportively kiss a pretty girl
tourist that he had just robbed of a gold bracelet.
He gallantly returned the bracelet to her and then
made off with the remaining plunder. He stole
a pinto broncho in getting across the country, the
broncho was recognized and he was arrested for
theft. When the sheriff captured him he took
it for granted that he was wanted for the stage-
robbery and gave himself away. The capture was
made and he was tried in Tulare County. He was
found guilty and convicted on March 16, 1874, and
sent up to serve a thirty-seven year sentence at
San Quentin. There he bore the prison number
of 11883. Twice in his prison career has he been
branded with the numbers: eleven and eight, his
Spokane County number being 1178. Are these
numbers significant of something that is mystical
and fatal and perhaps traditional?

In 1878 he was promoted to laundry trusty as
a reward due for his good behavior. He had deliberately made himself a record so that in time
he would have the coveted opportunity of short-
ening the sentence.

October the first he arrayed himself in the
warden's "very best," left his stripes, including

his stars behind with his compliments and escaped
the confinements of San Quentin. During the following days he hid and wandered at night, living
on fruit, but at the end of an uncomfortable week
he made the discouraging discovery that he had
not traveled twenty miles away. He stopped at a
ranch house near Petaluma one evening and
begged for a hand-out. The women invited him
into the kitchen and cooked him a lunch. They
did not suspect what a dangerous character they
were harboring in their humble little home, but
while he sat there ravenously devouring everything before him, William Brown, the owner of
the ranch, returned home and recognized in him
the escaped convict whom the authorities were
looking for, from a description circulated throughout the country.

He armed himself with a rifle and valiantly
took his stand between the convict and the door
When Downen had finished eating and rose to
leave he met the friendly looking rifle with a
characteristic sneer and Brown commanded him
to surrender.

"Not on your life, you d—— coward," he
shouted in his slurring voice as he picked up a
large lamp and without a pause or hesitation,
landed it on top of Brown's head.

The furious force of the blow knocked Brown down and uttering a boyish whoop of delight Downen leaped over his body and ran from the house. Brown unloaded his rifle in the direction of the vanishing convict, but as Brown was a bum shot he failed to hit him and Downen went merrily whistling ragtime on his way.

The broken lamp set fire to the delicate frame cottage and the roseate glow which ascended in wavering columns from out the groves of lemon trees reddened the evening sky and lighted the fugitive's escape.

Brown and his little family with their animals, stood in a disconsolate group in the glow of the radiating fire, helplessly witnessing all their earthly goods go up in smoke.

Downen then hit the high places and soon reached a small town, where he was welcomed most cordially by being shot in the neck by the hospitable night-watchman. He indignantly resented this familiarity, immediately saying goodbye and hit the trail again, this time headed for Sacramento. The night he arrived there the town was in an uproar because Policeman Hunt had been murdered, and Downen left town at once to avoid arrest on suspicion. He wearily wandered on to Truckee and traded a San Quentin blanket for a gun and then held up a tally-ho party.

They were a dilapidated crowd returning from a ranch where they had had an old-time dance in the barn. They were dirty and sleepy and just had enough in them to sing college songs to accompaniments of sacred music. Downen certainly looked diabolical to the hic-hic-hooray crowd and what he didn't get no one had.

Half an hour later he held up two business men, relieving them of change, jewelry, letters, private papers and everything else that happened to be in their raided pockets. He there heard that a Chinaman of Colfax had drawn two thousand dollars out of the local bank and was going to China with his savings.

Downen, without warning, interrupted his hop-dreams, which included an almond-eyed yellow girl all wound up in a marvelous kimono, who was waiting for him in the land of Celestial Peppers, as he was flopping along a lonely mountain trail and attempted to touch him for the two thousand, but the frightened Chink leaped headlong over a little bluff, landing on the slope below and rolled over and over down the hill. He kept on rolling at the rate of "A Limited," until he rolled into the bed of a dried-up creek at the

foot of the canyon and disappeared in the quick-
sand there. Whether or not he went straight on
through to China is not known, but Downen
didn't get a cent and anyway he did not consider
it worth while to follow him. Downen thereupon returned to Truckee, and as he had feared,
was arrested on suspicion of the Hunt murder.
As he was being captured he was shot in the leg,
the bullet could not be located, and he was left
with the complimentary souvenir of the event.

Fear of being lynched by the blood-thirsty
comrades of Policeman Hunt drove him to the
confession that he was an escaped convict, and
on December eleventh of the same year he was
returned to the gloomy depths of San Quentin
and one extra year added to his time as punish-
ment for escaping.

Number 11883 was fated to be returned to
his cell on the eleventh of December, which again
shows how magically destiny ordains who shall
win and who shall lose in the lottery of life by the
numbers with which each soul is branded, and the
number (eleven) must surely have been fatal to
Allen Hence Downen.

Special Agent Hume, of the Wells-Fargo Express Company, was at that time, for some unknown reason working for the pardon of Downen,

and through his power Governor Stoneman was induced to commute the sentence to ten years.

Maybe Agent Hume recognized something extraordinary in Downen's character which disinterested people would fail to notice, and maybe he had an instinctive knowledge that Downen was capable of something as rare and lustral as his crimes were hideous, anyway Hume had a reason and an honorable one which was not public business and therefore he failed to divulge. This sentence Downen served until he was liberated September 16, 1884.

From San Quentin he went to San Jose, California, and worked for a seedman there by the name of Maggett.

On the balmy night of June 7, 1885, he ventured out, determined to "stick some one up." In the beautiful park of St. James he met an elderly man who was leisurely strolling home after the game and enjoying the glory of the night in the wee-small hours. The burning end of the gentleman's cigar served as a maddening beacon to the frenzied convict. He looked like a haul worth while, and as Downen came face to face with him, he ordered: "Hands up."

The man, whose natural instinct was to reach for his revolver, made an almost unconscious movement in that direction and Downen shot him dead.   As the silent night melted into dawn and the red sun triumphantly rose over the scene a picture of tragedy was revealed to the eyes of the waking world.

A dead body was stretched across the road like a stain on a fluttering white ribbon.  The face that had coolly met everything from a midnight raid when the lid was on to being murdered; with grim humor, was motionless.  The keen, steady eyes whose devil-may-care smile had cheered broken gamblers on their feast and famine courses were closed.  The white face with the red blood staining the ruffled iron-gray hair told the story in itself.  (He's dead and gone, boys.).

He was known as "Hurricane Braun," he had earned that title through his periodical luck, and he could lose as gloriously as he could win, and sink back vanquished as bravely as he could conquer.  If the chips were his he sat up the drinks, and if someone else had won them, he drank to their health with the  following  characteristic toast:

"But the man who's a man won't forget he's a man 'though he's out on a h—— of a spree."

He had the rare distinction of being the most popular and wealthy citizen of San Jose.  Near his body was found the revolver with its one empty chamber, and the coroner's jury reached a verdict of, "Suicide without apparent motive."

A few days after the murder of Braun, and on the night of June 21, 1885, Downen attempted another hold-up in the same part of the park.

A young blood by the name of Dreschmayer, with two girls, Maggie Nihill and Molly Canavan, left Santa Clara in a buggy bound for San Jose, and had reached the famous Alameda when Downen stepped before the horse and ordered their hands up.

Dreschmayer undaunted, lashed the horse and passed the freebooter who fired at him. A bullet hit one of the girls and she screamed. Her agonized cries ring in his ears to this day, they strike a pang of remorse in his heart.

"Her cries haunt me—I hear them always. I never would have shot if I had thought there was a woman in the buggy, but the night was dark and I didn't see her. She was a catholic girl and suffered so long," Downen pathetically confessed eleven years later, eleven years, eleven again in his career.

"I heard that she died soon afterward and I'm awful sorry—I never meant to hurt her," he tenderly continued.

The shooting of the girl is the greatest regret of his life. Downen was not suspected, and the sentinel palms and daisy and wood-violet jeweled sod of St. James held and hid the secret. The mystery of Braun's death was buried with his mute lips under the granite memorial that marked the grave of a popular and beloved sport. The mystery of the hold-up soon afterward when he shot the girl was forgotten like a Bowery brawl that goes down in history on an illegible blotted page.

There but a stone's throw from the park that formed a picturesque background for these two fatal tragedies rises the towering Vendome against the spangled sky. The sleepy moon keeps its vigil over all and the myriad lights from the Vendome shine beaconingly through the gala pepper groves like the enchanted lamps of a far distant fairy palace, like the flickering tapers of a pagan altar where a goddess of beauty reigns and mirth and dancing and feasting and flirting inspire the devout worshipers. There on the other side the park is bordered by the Bowery scene of the Alameda.

A dirty row of dilapidated buildings that are known more or less from coast to coast for the tragedies enacted within their depths. The blank,

barren walls of the road house whose shaded
windows frown gloomily upon the flowery park of
St. James do not betray the crime that rages like
battle within its confines. The weather-beaten
roof and battered shutters do not reveal the elegance of the decorated interior.

It had once been a mission house in the infancy of the little, New World town, where the
pale-faced volunteers of the Salvation Army had
led regenerated heathens from out the lawlessness
of frontier life. Where sacred melodies once
sanctified the air, salacious carousal now holds
sway. Where the organ once stood now is the
polished bar, and the spacious door which once
welcomed the unfortunate, is the exit for the
drunken visitors—after they go broke.

There the highest and the lowest mingle in
lawless revelry. There women come face to face
with the battle of life, a one-sided battle wherein
the weaker have no weapons and fall, maimed and
branded forever, until death closes out the scenes
of life from their strained eyes and they come before a generous Judge who judges, by the strength
alone, with which the victims of destiny have
been endowed.

"The grave alone gives peace."

There time is forgotten by the merry

denizens who go thoughtlessly on their ways, forgetting the Alameda which is an underworld stepping stone to something better or worse.

Within those mute walls the game is at a fever heat, breaking and making the players, who are helpless instruments in the relentless hands of fate.

Yes, the Alameda is famous, and so is the Vendome; one a brilliant dive, the other a social palace. The inflorescent surroundings of the Vendome do not correspond with their neighbor, the Alameda, whose muddy walks lead human feet into the vortex of what?

There, where the Bowery rages, are numerous gambling holes, cafes, saloons, dens, haunts and buildings, whose very quietude means revel and whose revel means ruination.

Was it sentiment that led the rough Missourian to the park of St. James for the sport of "sticking someone up," and was it romance, unnursed and unacknowledged, that made the terrorized cries of the wounded girl that rang through the park and the Bowery, haunt the convict? Whatever it was no one can say; perhaps Downen knows, but that is another mystery in his life.

Shortly after this Downen met a Mexican

woman whose luring visage was more on the order of a witch than the tragical beauty displayed by the fairer sisters of her half-breed race. But she had some money and Downen flattered her, and lived with her, and robbed her, all in his dare-devil manner. The woman, whose feverish red blood drove her to hate as bitter as her love had been passionate, turned on him and he was arrested and tried on a charge of grand larceny in Santa Clara county. The verdict was guilty, and he was convicted to seven years' durance at San Quentin on October 17, 1885.

He escaped with some other desperate prisoners September 12, 1889, but fell from a ladder on the prison wall and broke his right ankle. With excruciating pain and in dire want, yet undaunted, he trailed through the underbrush, but within a week he was recaptured and tried in Marin county for escaping, and two months more were added to his time. When he realized how seriously he was injured he made his two comrades leave him behind and escape themselves. With their aid there would have been a good chance of Downen escaping with them, but he would not let them risk being caught to help him. Here his unselfish nature predominated and he alone answered for them all. He was locked up

again in San Quentin and nursed in the sick
ward until his ankle got well, but, nevertheless,
it left him lame for life. When the doctors ex-
amined it they told him that if he did not have
it amputated he would die, and he said: "I'll
take my chance; when I die I want to die whole
and not by degrees." In reality he was thankful for the chance of dying. He most reluctantly
served out his sentence, and was discharged
December 18, 1892.

He immediately ventured north to Spokane,
where he resumed the operations of his trade
in a systematic way, and went by the name of
J. H. Lewis. He accomplished many jobs, big
and little, but finally was landed. At the time
of his arrest he was a cabby for one of the
leading liveries in Spokane.

One night he drove a hack for a rich man
who was out on a spree with another man's wife.
The woman was covered with diamonds and the
man's pockets were bulging with money.

The night was dense and stormy, and they
ordered him to drive to a well-known resort on
an isolated road. He disobeyed the order and
drove past the outskirts of the city. When he
had reached a deserted building that in former
days had been a road house, but was then con-

demned as haunted, he stopped and ordered the man and woman out of the hack. To their amazement they found themselves on a road that apparently led off to nowhere, with only the barren prairie and the solitary haunted house confronting them.

The man whipped out a minature revolver that was only a sad excuse of a firearm, with which he had prepared himself in case of an encounter with the woman's husband. Downen promptly took it away from him.

Downen stripped the woman of her jewels and emptied the man's pockets at the point of his own full-grown revolver, and after a hasty examination to see if he had overlooked anything, he told them to go to h—— and drove back to civilization.

They were left with their choice of three things; to stay out in the storm all night, to take refuge in the haunted house or return to town in the tracks of the rapidly disappearing hack by foot. Which of the three they did is not recorded; maybe they availed themselves of the rare opportunity of watching for spooks in the lonely building, maybe they trudged back to town, but when they did arrive in Spokane they reported on the driver who was complacently smoking a cigar at the stable and waiting for an assignment.

The whole affair then leaked out; it was too good to be kept, and a scandel in which a club man and a society woman figured was turned over to the press, and the dailies were yellow with it. Society pretended to be shocked, fellow clubmen pretended to be mad, women gloried in it at pink teas, but the only ones that imagined themselves injured was the clubman's wife and the society woman's husband.

It was a choice bit of notoriety that was effervescent and intoxicated the colony of temperance society whose systematic existences let in very little real life.

Downen was tried and sentenced to two years in the pen of Spokane county on January 18, 1893. His number there was 1178, and he served this sentence and was discharged October 28, 1894.

His mother about this time went to Helena, Montana, to make a new home, and he accompanied her there. She was white haired and feeble from the sorrow he had caused her. She begged and pleaded with him to abandon his restless roving and settle down to an honest life and care for her in her numbered days. With all the mock chivalry peculiar of his type he promised, and a few hours after pledging a solemn vow to this effect, the votary broke into a jewelry store in Park county. He emptied the cases and then fired the safe, but before he could rob it, he heard someone approaching who had been attracted by the blasting. As the police forced in the front door he disappeared with his bag of plunder through the back window. The police went after him in his own tracks, but the night was dark and he escaped. The haul amounted to about one thousand five hundred dollars.

He wandered away in the dead of night to a burial ground, near Livingston, and hid the plunder. As time wore on and the police were unable to trace the jewelry or the freebooter Downen felt safe in disposing of it, but he had forgotten where he had buried it and was never able to locate the stuff.

He then spent some time in Ogden, Salt Lake and Cheyenne.

He came to Denver in the spring of 1895 and obtained work on the ranch of A. R. McCool, which was located near Henderson station. He at once commenced his operations along the Sand Creek road and became popularly known as the gentlemanly Sheridan Boulevard robber who was too clever to be caught. He bought a wheel, and after work every night rode into Denver and Brighton to "stick someone up."

One night in May, T. J. Boyer, whose ranch lays in a fertile strata west of Riverside cemetery, was giving an old-time blow out, where champagne ran like water. His numerous guests made merry in a whole-hearted, truly Western way.

Most of them turned in on the improvised beds on the garret floor, but a traveling man by the name of W. A. Hopkins, decided to return to Denver, owing to important business which would demand his attention early in the morning.

Downen met him out near Elyria, and all he possessed was a battered gold watch, a few dollars and a new overcoat, all of which Downen appropriated.

His next robbery occurred six nights later when he took a watch, gun and overcoat from J. R. McDonald, who was out driving with Sadie Slarton of Rocky Mountain lake; these he sold to a second-hand dealer.

After this he went back to McCool's ranch and stayed until July 3, when the patriotic spirit inspired him to go forth and celebrate by blowing

ALLEN HENCE DOWNEN

off the top of someone's head. He came to Denver and commenced his celebrations in the Highlands. His cool nerve and daring confidence astonished the citizens, who were never quick enough to get the drop on him, and in 1896 he made forty or fifty hauls in Denver and Brighton.

One morning two popular business and society men were returning to Denver with three women of the tenderloin. The sun was gaily rising, but the hilarious occupants of the carriage were feeling too good to notice such trifling matters. The team of glossy bays was galloping along the Highland road, unguided, when Downen's masked figure caught hold of the bridle and brought them to a sudden stop. Their dissonant songs ceased as they opened their eyes and dumbly realized that someone else was master of the situation, whose invigorating sensations were composed of green lizard phantoms and painful realities in which they saw stars.

Downen helped himself to everything he could find on them; he didn't find much, for this was their second trimming. The revolver, he threateningly brandished, appeared to them like a war cannon, and after an interesting search of their pockets, he informed them that it was time to go home and sent them on their way hardly knowing whether they had really been robbed or if the road-house brand was responsible for it all.

He then did three of the cleverist, most novel jobs recorded on the Sand Creek road. Everything that Downen ever did in that line was novel and original.

He stopped a man and a woman in a buggy, taking fourteen dollars from the man and every penny he had, but gallantly scorned the idea of taking the woman's diamonds.

He later held up three men that were broke, on the outskirts of Denver, and what souvenirs he got from them he never told.

His most audacious robbery was the next in order, when he held up the Highlands Dairy wagon. This he robbed of fifty dollars, put H. M. Keever, the driver, out and took the milk wagon and drove into Denver, depositing forty dollars of the stolen money in the First National bank to his own credit.

The same night he approached three men and a woman on the Golden road. They were society swells and he took everything they had, except the woman's make-up. The last he saw of them the demolished woman was indulging in

a cat-fit and the men had a mild form of hydro-
phobia.

During this time, very frequently he met
Sheriff Kelly, who was out looking for him, and
once, he says, he had a notion to "stick the sheriff
up," just for fun.

Then, on the night of July 22nd, he entered
the saloon on the Sand Creek road and sat down
in the shadow to rest. While he sat there, Michael
White, who was a Kansas Pacific locomotive
engineer, and Charles Fetta, with two women,
dropped in for a drink. The jolly party had been
out dove hunting. The sport had been good, so
it was late when they entered the saloon on their
return home. The bartender complimented White
on his fine watch, and White proudly boasted of
its value. From the conversation Downen over-
heard he concluded that they would be good ones
to "stick up." He quietly left the saloon and
walked up the hill. In a few minutes the hunters
came riding along, weary after their hard day of
sport, and it turned from dove-shooting into man-
shooting.

Downen ordered them to halt, which they
answered by firing, swearing and driving on, and
then in his madness to kill them, Downen only
succeeded in riddling White's leg full of bullets.

To save White's life it was necessary to amputate the leg.

The next afternoon a woman was driving a sleepy horse back into the country, alone, after purchasing provisions in Denver. Downen stopped her, and searched her, but found nothing.

"Take the groceries, take the horse, take everything, but, oh; don't kill me," she wailed.

"I won't, but don't be so d—— sentimental about it," he impatiently retorted.

The Sand Creek road and Sheridan boulevard hold-ups were by this time getting on the nerves of the police, so July 23rd, when the woman breathlessly telephoned headquarters that the robber was at large, Chief Russell and Captain Tuttle decided to go forth and be held-up by the bold highwayman in order to capture him. They considered the night a very favorable one for such a venture, and hurriedly hitched the chief's favorite stallion to a light buggy.

The horse and both officers were in jubilent spirits as they dashed away to Sheridan boulevard, but they were greeted as they entered it by a masked figure, who darted from under a large maple tree into the road before them. The officers were taken totally unawares by the sudden encounter of the man they were after.

"Hands up," shouted Downen.

"Hands up, yourself," replied Chief Russell.

"I'll be d—— if I do, you —— —— ——,"
the Missourian's slurring voice rang out reckless-
ly, as he opened fire at them, recognizing instantly
who he was dealing with.

Chief Russell rolled out of the back of the
buggy, and Tuttle tumbled out some other way,
and they both returned fire.

A shot from Downen's gun enterd the quivering shoulder of the blooded beast, causing it to
plunge wildly forward.

In the breathless moment, the rig had been
carried past Downen, and he had perforated it
with bullets, in a vain effort to hit the chief
and captain. They returned the compliment by
firing as he was beating a hasty retreat into the
shadow of the night.

When Chief Russell and Tuttle had bravely
left headquarters to be held-up they had felt con-
fident, that together, they could master the lone
freebooter which they ingloriously failed to do
and bitterly lamented the fact that they had not
taken the whole department along.

The police and detective force had been crazy
at their failure to capture the robber and Russell's

and Tuttle's failure which rewarded a valiant attempt, incensed them to a more critical tension.

The wounded animal died a few moments later with noble intelligence. The hands that had driven him to destruction had been those of his doting master and he succumbed to the fatal wound in his own loyal, silent way.

Russell and Tuttle were forced to abandon the rig and rode back to town in a car, disheartened and feeling delicate about meeting the force with the news that their pet had fallen under the fire of the man who was too quick to be caught.

Downen too, rode to town in the same car and was not recognized by the officers because he had shed his mask.

He sat in the seat behind them all the way and inwardly gloried in their failure.

Nothing that Downen had ever done in his life from "sticking good ones up" to murder affected the hearts of the entire police and detective department as the brutal killing of Chief Russell's prancing pet. It struck a pang of regret and sentiment that those surviving the old days still feel and no matter what the hand of the law could do for Downen, they could never forget or forgive that one brutal act.

If the incident is recalled to big, jovial Chief

Russell pathos saddens his eyes and you listen to a tender reminiscence of the wonderful joy-rides he had in olden days when his fleet-footed pet dashed away through the teeming heart of Denver town to the fires that swept away the crude 'though picturesque landmarks that years and years before had arisen out of a buffalo stamping-ground and a proud pleasure that restrospection kindles glows in his face as he confides how the thrilling magnetism of the animated horse tingled in his veins.

Downen laid off for awhile and took a little vacation after slaughtering the animal that was the pride of the force. The wrath of the police boiled high and he knew that they would revengefully resort to almost impossible measures for the satisfaction of his capture.

After that he saw Marshal McNeil and his crowd out looking for him, they were not ten feet away and they did not even notice him.

He then resumed operations along the Sand Creek road.

The first hold-up of his series occurred near Rocky Mountain Lake and Mrs. W. J. Wagner and Mrs. J. Webb were the heroines. He stopped their horse, ordered them out and thoroughly searched them. He unearthed some money and jewelrv and after looking it over, returned it all to them, begging their pardon.

He then boldly entered a car on the Denver, Lakewood and Golden Line and held up Conductor F. S. Logan, getting fifteen dollars and a gold watch, the latter he tossed into a pig-pen near the tracks and with the money took a trip to Evans.

In his next robbery a little boy kindled his sympathy.

While Downen was robbing his father the kid jumped out of the back of the buggy and ran across the fields. Downen ran after him.

"I didn't mean to hurt him but felt sorry for him and wanted to put him back in the buggy."

The boy reached home first and told his sick mother that his father had been killed on the road. The false report so affected her that she became an invalid.

Out on the lonely moonlit road near Riverside Cemetery he stopped two dudes who were driving a spirited young horse at break-neck speed.

As he expressed it, "They had fits."

All they had were some choice cigarettes, which Downen took anyway for meanness. They hardly knew whether he was a genuine holdup or an apparition, resurrected from one of the near-by graves. Anyway, they let him have his way and their cigarettes for fear that they, too, would rest beneath the foreboding tombstones in the cemetery.

Robert L. Cain, with his very best, Mrs. Lammers, was enjoying the distant mountain scenery which rose against the horizon under the transfiguring light of the moon like silver clouds when Downen curtly interrupted their romantic reveries and helped himself to all they had.

He thanked them for the plunder and then cursed them.

The profanity he wasted was of the brand, with variations, that is known only in the sacred sanctums of the Bowery joints back in Missouri, and was so multifarious as to be impossible to repeat had they been loaded enough to desire to.

He then held-up a milk wagon three consecutive times, only securing four dollars in all.

He shot at and hit a man who had his girl out driving, the wounded man fell down into the bottom of the buggy and as Downen puts it: "I guessed he was dead."

He then met a girl with a little boy on a lonely road and what he got from them is not accurately known, but when Downen took a watch from the kid he had to give it back because he felt so bad about it. Here again sympathy was unearthed by the tears of a little boy. Downen must have had some tender feeling for little children which he never explained.

The last murder which he was given credit for occurred on June 27, 1896, and Joel W. Ashworth was the victim. Ashworth had spent the evening taking a street car ride with a young lady friend of his wife's who was at that time absent from the city. He and his wife had quarreled and she had left home shortly before his murder.

Ashworth was walking along Curtis street. It was ten o'clock and he had reached Twenty-fifth street when a masked man stepped out of the shadow, at the same instant ordering, "Hands up."

Ashworth, unintimidated made a movement to strike the thug with his cane and was shot dead.

A bullet entered his skull a few inches above his right ear, viciously eviscerating his brains.

The next morning the bullet was found in the gutter, matted in a particle of bloody hair and was preserved as a possible clue.

Ashworth fell to the pavement unconscious and was removed to the County Hospital where he died at five in the morning without regaining consciousness. No loved one was at his bedside as he broke the ties of life, only the mute nurses and professional men witnessed his final hours. It was generally thought that Mrs. Ashworth's lover had taken that means of getting Ashworth out of the way. He was a valued representative of the Western Meat and Livestock Company of Denver.

There was nothing on his person with which to identify him and it was not unil he was missed at the business house that James Guard and J. M. McCabe, his bosses, recognized his body at the morgue.

A woman and a little girl were the sole witnesses of the murder although the residents of that neighborhood plainly heard the shot, that without warning, ended the life of a human being.

The woman saw the thug escape and could tell nothing more.

Ashworth's fellow lodgemen offered a reward of two hundred and fifty dollars for the scalp of the man who had called one from out their ranks.

It was on Sunday evening about a quarter after seven when he robbed Tom Sullivan, the postmaster of Henderson Station.

A placid moon shed its light over the tranquil scene; the same old moon that sees all and betrays nothing.

Sullivan was enjoying an after dinner smoke when he was abruptly called from his store by

Downen. Sullivan had known him only as a laborer that sometimes hung around his store with others of the same official occupation. Sullivan invited Downen in but he refused, asking him to help him load a trunk at the depot.

Sullivan re-entered his store and arming himself with a revolver unhesitatingly accompanied Downen.

When they had turned a corner Sullivan looked up at his companion and was astonished to find his face concealed under a black mask. An ugly looking revolver was aimed at his eyes and a cool voice whispered confidently in his ear, "Be quiet and don't make a d—— fool of yourself or I'll," the whisper died in an unspoken though well understood threat.

Two tramps at that moment happened along and paused like children, interested in the hold-up.

Downen turned his gun in their direction, at the same time keeping Sullivan covered and ordered them to throw up their hands and stand back of the postmaster.

He then relieved Sullivan of sixteen dollars and fifty cents, a gold watch and his dangerous pet, the revolver.

Then he took a piece of rope from his pocket

and tied Sullivan's hands behind his back. He had purchased the rope at Sullivan's store.

With profane orders to stand still and not to move away from the spot until it was time to open the postoffice the next morning and letting Sullivan feel the friendly muzzle of a revolver against his throbbing temple, Downen took the two tramps in charge and started down the road toward Denver.

Walking ties was too slow and besides out of his line so when the sociable trio had traveled a few hundred yards nearer to civilization Downen stopped and shook hands with the tramps.

"Here, take this," he said, handing them each a silver dollar.

"Don't squeal pards," he familiarly pleaded.

"We three are all the same, aren't we?"

"Good luck to you," he continued, grasping their dirty hands again and then he started on a mad stampede across a field of clover and that was the very last that the wayfarers saw of him.

He unearthed a wheel from out of the underbrush and rode into Denver, but on his way he met a farmer who was hauling a load of hay.

Downen made the ignorant countryman climb down from his throne on top of the golden harvest and searched him.

The sentimental youth had the picture of a girl in his pocket and that was all Downen got. She was pretty and he took the picture for a keepsake. The hay was no good to him so he shook hands with the tearful boy and went on his way.

The farmer unhitched one of his horses and rode madly into Henderson to report the tragedy. In Henderson he heard of the robbery of Sullivan and they telegraphed the Denver police with the information that a daring robber had held up the postmaster and taken a photograph from a vindictive farmer and was riding a wheel toward Denver.

The police thereupon gave his description to every local bicycle shop and at one-thirty p. m. on October 19th he turned up at a shop on Stout street to have his tires pumped up.

The manager detained him and telephoned headquarters.

Five minutes later Detective Harry Burlew, who is now one of the most prominent business men of Denver and whose honor is his trade mark, appeared upon the scene and showing Downen his star marched him down to the Chief.

Downen made a half-effort to resist the detective but after a full glance into Burlew's resolute eyes he realized it was no use. Burlew's strong personality invariably impresses people with a singular force that at once makes him master of any situation. He had arrested Downen for robbery and locked him up. A twinkle of mirth filled the genial detective's eyes as he vehemently declared that it was not for robbing Sullivan that he had arrested him but for taking the Idyllic keepsake from the love-lorn farmer.

Downen spent a very restless night, not sleeping for more than ten minutes at a time.

Perhaps remorse awoke in his heart, perhaps he heard the cries of a wounded girl ringing far away in the gilded West and maybe their echoes faintly penetrated the prison walls to where his feverish head tossed to and fro upon the narrow pillow.

But maybe the vision of a character of the slums haunted him, maybe the wild-eyed half-clad Artie Dallas filled his dreams, the frail dissipated girl who once had been tragically beautiful and loved him with a loyalty that she alone was capable of, was dreaming of him. She was the one person in the world that knew his life, to her it had been revealed like a blood-thirsty panorama and she had forgiven him for it all because he loved her so perfectly and his secrets were inviolable and buried in her brain. She carried his

burden in silence with the sorrowful burden of
her own life that had been squandered in the deep-
est dregs of what God had created to be mystically
beautiful.

And the thought of another woman of the
Bowery may have troubled him, the big handsome
Swedish girl; Rosie Olson may have brazenly
flaunted her dash and vigor in his imagination.
The languorous gray eyes in the creamy, blushing face with its crown of tawny hair may have
taunted him and her mellow voice may have
whispered in his dream: "Oh, you wanted, you
devil, but you didn't, for I got away."

He did not love her, he hated her, for he
loved her little friend, Artie Dallas, and perhaps
he longed to spill the blood of Rosie Olson upon
the altar of sacrifice.

Some unconfessed thing refused him rest,
some crime undone mocked him or the cries of a
girl rang like a warning echo of the past in his
ears for he was madly pacing his cell as dawn
shed its lurid glow upon his haggard face.

In the morning, bright and early, Chief Russell entered his office and ordered that a hearty
breakfast be served to Downen. This order was
promptly obeyed and the prisoner gratefully received it. Then the good natured chief ordered

that Downen be given a cigar. Downen **eagerly** smoked the cigar and then he was **summoned to** the chief's private sanctum.

"Good morning Chief," he called as **he bright-**ly greeted the officer.

"Good morning Downen," responded the Chief, hale and hearty.

Downen then thanked the Chief **for his** thoughtful kindness.

The Chief, in a warm friendly manner **asked** Downen a few questions which he answered **with** sullen silence.

He carried on like a stubborn, defiant **broncho** and when asked his address he promptly **named a** Larimer street rooming house. Detectives **were** immediately dispatched to the place and **learned** that he had misled them. They returned **and re-**ported on their trip and Downen was accused **of** deceit. He made no answer, raised no plea in defense but resolutely refused to be **cross-exam-**ined and was led back to his cell and locked up. Detectives were then put on the case and finally, after four hours search, they located **a shanty at** 1935 Arapahoe street, where Downen really **did** steadily hire a room. They forced in the **door and** hurriedly returned to headquarters with **two valu-**able gold watches; one bore a Masonic emblem **on** its fob while from the tempered case of the other smiled a girl's dimpled face. They also brought one gun, three masks and numerous articles necessary to his mysterious profession with two locked valises.

On a ring of keys that had been taken from Downen's pockets when he was locked up were two keys belonging to the valises, which they opened. In one of them they found a large forty-five caliber Hopkins and Allen revolver; no heart beat within its stout barrel, no soul pleaded for compassion; it was as mechanical as the man who used it with which to kill fellow beings.

A few more masks, a pint of chloroform, a quart of whiskey and a varied assortment of jewelry were found in the valises. Then there was a neat little package of letters; some from his loving sister, one from his brother, General Downen, pleading with him to settle down to something honest, which in time he would be proud of, and some tender little love notes from his faithful Artie.

After lunch Chief Russell summoned him again. Captain Tuttle and Detective Burlew were with the chief. Downen came before the officers with defiant determination. His vicious jaws were set and his sullen eyes downcast.

"Where did you get this, Downen?" said the chief, as he held up the watch with the Masonic charm.

"It's none of your d—— business," he angrily blurted out.

"Yes it is," replied the naturally unruffled chief, as he held up the other watch and asked, "Who is she?" The girl's face smiled out of the gold case.

"Don't know," said Downen.

"Well, I'm sorry for your sister; she's not like you, but this IS a dandy." He held up the Hopkins and Allen revolver.

"You've got me dead to rights, boys, and I give in," Downen muttered through his gold teeth.

Russell, whose stallion he had slaughtered, brightened up under this admission, and Detective Burlew and Captain Tuttle eagerly listened.

"I shot your horse, Chief; you couldn't get over it, could you?"

"But you are not a very good shot," he tauntingly laughed to Tuttle.

"You did not win any medals that night," Tuttle returned.

"If I had known that you fellows were out of ammunition I would have stayed and killed you both," he said, as his hand fell to his waist, where a belt of cartridges had always been on duty.

No third degree was necessary to bring this prisoner to a complete confession.

"I know you have got me cinched, and as you can send me up for robbing Sullivan I have determined to make a clean breast of everything. Life has been a d—— failure to me and I am a dangerous enemy to society. I would as soon kill a man that would resist me when I would try to rob him as to smoke a cigar."

With a half bitter, half dangerous laugh and a defiant flash of his cold gray eyes to Detective Burlew, who had arrested him, he said, "It's lucky for you that I didn't have my gun with me or you never would have taken me alive."

Here he broke down and required stimulants before Chief Russell could continue the examination.

"Did you kill Ashworth?" the chief asked him then.

Downen smiled grimly, almost humorously, as he replied, "Yes."

"But I am sorry I did it. I didn't like to, but thought it best. There is the gun that did the work. I bought it at Solomon's three-ball shop. It's a beauty and has faced many a duck. I am sorry I killed Ashworth, but I am dead sorry I did not kill Tom Sullivan. He deserved to be dead, and if I had I wouldn't be here today."

"Am I afraid to kill? Not much," he scoffed at the idea.

"I would have no more scruples about shooting one of you gnetlemen down in cold blood at this moment than I would about lighting a cigar, and if I had that there gun I'd show you that I mean it d—— quick. Seventeen years of the lockup have spoiled me. If I had been given a light sentence in the first place I might have reformed, but I can't do it now, it's too late. I am ready for the gallows. I don't want to be tried and will plead guilty to it all now, and I don't want to see no judges or juries or reporters or anything else. All I want is to die right now. But I tell you, Mr. Burlew, if you had tried to get me today and if I'd had my gun along with me, one of us would be at the morgue. I never would have been guilty of letting any man take me without shooting me down. You've got me dead, boys, and I give in."

When asked the particulars of the Ashworth murder, he brightly and readily responded:

"I felt pretty blue. I was dead broke and desperate and concluded to go out and stick up someone that Saturday night. I walked back and forth between Twenty-fifth and Twenty-sixth streets, on Curtis, waiting for someone to come along. Lord knows how long I had waited when I saw Ashworth. There was no one else on the street except two women, who were a long ways back of him. I meant to hold them up too when they came along. Well, I met Ashworth on the corner and shoved my gun in his face. He resisted me and I shot him down, but I'm d—— sorry. I ran away from him when he fell. I didn't stop to search him, but I ran up Twenty-sixth street to the alley and then went bumming it around town."

"Did you go to see Artie Dallas that night?" Chief Russel asked.

A tender smile passed over the prisoner's face, such a transient vagary of sentiment.

"Yes, I went to her," he purred, "but early in the morning I went back to McCool's ranch and waited," he thoughtfully answered.

"When I heard that you had no clue I came back to town. Oh, I kept posted. You never did get the drop on me before," he lamented, his hand again touching his empty hip pocket.

"I'm dead sorry you caught me yesterday," he said to Detective Burlew. "I wish it were today instead, and then Rosie Olson would be dead. Yes, the wine rooms would have given up her body to the morgue. Rosie would be silent if it were only today. I meant to kill her sure last night. The night before last I took her to the theatre to see a tragedy, some famous historical rot, and I went home with her. She is Artie's chum. Artie was out of town. She had gone up to Cripple Creek for a few days. After the show was out Rosie and I went down to the Arcade, on Larimer street. It was late when we left there, after eating and drinking and carousing. She lives at the Phoenix block, and I tried all night long to get away with her, but she got wise to me and kept the light burning. I put a chair beside the bed and spread my handkerchief out on it. When I thought she had fallen off to sleep I poured chloroform on the handkerchief and went to put it over her mouth, but she woke up. She went to the hospital not long ago and had an operation. She had been given chloroform there and the smell of it woke her up. She opened her eyes like she was frightened and said to me, 'Oh, I smell chloroform.'

" 'No you don't, you're drunk, that's what's the matter. Go to sleep,' I told her, and she believed me and did.

"When she went to sleep I poured some more chloroform on the handkerchief and tried it again, but it woke her up.

" 'I smell chloroform,' she yelled.

" 'No you don't, Rosie; you're dreaming,' I told her, and she went off to sleep again.

"I poured all the chloroform that was in the bottle on the handkerchief then and was just putting it over her face when the smell woke her up again.

" 'My God! my God, it's chloroform,' she shrieked, as she jumped out of bed and ran from the room, locking me in. Oh, she suspected me all right. I was afraid to shoot her there in that block. I didn't want to make the noise and raise the house.

"Why did I want to kill her?" he repeated.

"Oh, she knew too d—— much about me— I was afraid she'd squeal. Artie Dallas knows everything; I know I can trust her, but I was afraid of Rosie Olson. She sure would be dead today, though, if you hadn't caught me yesterday. I had it all planned out when you interfered. I have only three regrets. The first is that I shot the girl in San Jose; I hear her cries now—always. My second regret is that I didn't kill Sullivan, and the third is that I didn't have

the chance to kill Rosie Olson. If I could only
have killed Sullivan and that d—— woman I
would be free today. But as the old proverb goes,
A pitcher always goes to the well once too often.'
And then, besides, I was a fool to keep the masks
and booty in my room, but it's too late now.
You've got me dead to rights. I had some more
jobs all planned out, too. I was going to attend
to them this week. First of all I intended to kill
Rosie Olson, then Tom Sullivan and rob his store
and post office at Henderson, then Marks Morris'
general store and Tom McCool's ranch, but it's all
off now, isn't it?" he said with a grim smile.

"Yes, at last," responded Chief Russell wearily.

Just then a letter was brought in for Downen.
It was from Mrs. Howard, his favorite niece, who
lived at Lakeport, Cal. It was an affectionate
letter, and in it she lovingly thanked him for sending her his picture. He broke down and wept,
every muscle in his gaunt frame quivering.

"Write on it 'Opened by mistake,' and send
it back," he pleaded. "I never want her to know
about me."

He was then shown an execution and judg-
ment on an old bond which recalled his first crime,
and tears again filled his eyes. It was on the

bond which was forfeited when he skipped West
to California, after murdering Townsend and
stealing Twombly's mule.

He then told Chief Russell that there were
five (5) years of mystery in his life which he had
not confessed and would not unless he were hung.
Just before going to the gallows he promised to
confide the inviolable secrets of those five years
to the chief.  As he was never hung, Chief Russell is still in ignorance concerning them, and in
an interview the writer had with him in April,
1911, at the penitentiary at Canon City, he still
maintained that that secret would go to the grave
with him; his refusal was final.

In those sacred years there may have been
a romance which is locked in the penetralia of
his heart; a romance that was too tender to repeat and only the silent stars bore witness of.  Did
he confide that secret to Artie Dallas?

She may have been with him in her girlhood
during those years, and it may have been her
love which made them so sacred to him.  It was
generally thought here that the liason between
them had been engendered in the Market street
wine rooms, where unfortunates like Artie Dallas
took refuge, and bunco men, curbstone brokers
and freebooters hung out.

But perhaps that general supposition was wrong. They may have met under the most ethical and lustral conditions and went down, volunteers to the dregs of the slums, hand in hand.

Those years of mystery may hold the secret of the awakening of their mutual love, which was so infinite that time and environment failed to weaken its ardor.

After retrospectively making this conditional promise to Chief Russell, the votary said that he had nothing more to confess at present, and was put back in his cell.

On December 3, 1896, he was tried before Judge Butler. He had no lawyer, for he needed none. He simply pleaded guilty and begged for a speedy sentence of death. Judge Butler was not satisfied with Downen appearing for himself and appointed Attorney Robert E. Foot to conduct his case.

His life story was repeated to the jury just as he had confessed it, repeated at its best and at its worst, his grewsome deeds frowning out of the shadow of the past, his little betrayals of sentiment touching the jury, and his voluntary confession of all winning their respect in a singular manner.

"I'm dead tired of life; I've had a hard one

and I want to die," he frankly admitted in his natural blunt way.

Downen sank back in the witness chair, that same old sullenness clouding his drawn features. Then a quiescence of resignation and the sullen gloom had drifted into a tearful hope that he would be condemned to death.

Sixty-three seconds elapsed while the jury was deliberating, and at the end of that short time they returned.

The head of the host of dignified men stood before the silent judge and slowly read the verdict.

A pall had settled over the room, the judge and spectators were apprehensive of the pending toll of death; only one face greeted the sentence cheerfully and that was the face of the multimurderer himself.

"Guilty of murder in the first degree!"

An agonized shriek rent the air. It was like an impassioned cry from the other world. The vibrating echo died away and the hushed spectators in the crowded court room breathed again.

A woman, as wildly sinuous as an animal, with tragical black eyes flashing from her pale face and her loosened dark hair falling about her bare throat, staggered forward.

She was bareheaded and scantily clad for the dead of winter, and a wild hopelessness deposed all other expressions from her face.

"Artie," Downen's hoarse shout expressed intense feeling.

The startled black eyes of Artie Dallas tenderly rebuked him for voluntarily confessing to the crimes that would take him to the gallows or the penitentiary. As she blindly stumbled toward him through the curious crowd, he suddenly awakened to the wrong he had done her by confessing, and he weakened when he realized the magnitude of her love.

With that old relevant bravado and dauntless reliance, he turned to the judge and jury and disavowed the statements he had made. He disclaimed every mysterious crime that he had deliberately related and proclaimed himself innocent.

But they had been verified, and it was too late.

"You voluntarily confessed to all these crimes that have convicted you, you pleaded guilty and asked for a speedy sentence of death, and you were satisfied until you saw Artie Dallas," the energetic prosecuting attorney put in.

"I knew you could not trace the murderer of Ashworth; I knew I could claim that crime, for

I am dead tired of durance, and in order to get death at your hands I accused myself, but I did not kill him. I spent that night with a woman. Neither did I kill the sport in San Jose; he committed suicide, and Ashworth was killed by a jealous lover of his wife's."

The trembling woman of the slums sank in the murderer's arms like a maimed wild bird.

"Artie," he purred.

Her limp body lay heavily against him and no answer came from her white lips. Artie had swooned.

They laid her frail body upon a couch by an open window. Her motionless face lay back upon its pillow of tangled dark hair like the face of a dead slave of the Orient who had been tortured to death. Had chains been around her slender wrists, had her feet been bare and bleeding, had her body been burnt in sacrifice, that tragical visage could not have bewrayed more violent anguish.

Downen broke away from his guards and shouldered his way to her. He gathered her up and clung to her with all the furious strength that despair commands.

He believed that she was dead, and did not express his feelings, whether he rejoiced for her sake or grieved for his, but he passionately caressed the marble-like face.

"Artie, Artie, Artie," he purred, in a voice so low but penetrating that it seemed capable of waking the dead.

The woman's wild eyes slowly opened and she joyously kissed him, for the fleeting moment forgetting that they were doomed to part, forgetting that the judge and jury and spectators were witnessing their valediction. Her temples were feverish and her eyes burned, for she had passed the stage of tears. All through the long trial she had rebelliously witnessed the secrets of his life, that had been so sacredly guarded by her in the shrine of her devotion, being vivisected for the inspection of the jury. There, way back in the court room, she had sobbed like a mourner at a funeral with a shawl drawn down over her bent head. Now that he was convicted of murder in the first degree, she had a vague prescience that she had not long to live on in her lawless way.

They clung together as if the parting meant death. Their hearts were united in a fusion of love which was so completely tempered that nothing earthly could mollify it, but the insoluble hand of the law abruptly interrupted their love scene and they were forcibly torn apart.

"Good-bye, little Artie," Downen tenderly called out to her. "Don't worry about me, try to forget."

Artie Dallas struggled under the iron grip of the deputy who held her back, and the pain in her wild black eyes mutely answered, "I never can."

A beautiful Swedish girl, in an enveloping fur coat, with diamonds in her pink ears and her yellow hair waving under her picture hat, laughed at him as he was led away.

Her white teeth gleamed like pearls between her rosy lips and her gloved finger was pointed at him.

"Oh, you can't hurt me now, can you? I'm safe at last."

A mellow laugh rippled, and Rosie Olson turned and swept from the room.

Downen went to the bare prison cell; Artie Dallas climbed three flights of dark stairs up to a cold, cheerless room, and Rosie Olson entered her luxurious suite.

All night Downen dreamed of the slender dark-eyed woman whom he loved. She was so true that there was no one to compare with her in all the world.

All night in her dingy room Artie suffered,

ROSIE OLSON

her body beat against the confining walls as if they had been a prison, and her feverish head burned. She dreamed of him through the long night, when she was asleep and when she was awake, and those dreams must surely have found him and comforted him as he lay on his prison cot.

Rosie Olson sat in the cheery glow of the fire in her rooms, with her silken kimono wound around her and her tawny hair hanging down over her creamy shoulders. A cigarette was between her lips and a bottle of wine and fragments of a lunch were on a stool beside her. She was contented, and had forgotten about Downen in his cell and Artie Dallas in her gloomy room, and Rosie deliriously dreamed delicious things as she puffed her cigarette, sipped her wine and cooed to her lover.

For twenty-five days the prisoner waited for the death sentence, and on December 28, 1896, he was sentenced to be hung in the third week of January, 1897.

There was no state law for hanging at that time, and the district attorney reconsidered the case and brooded over its outcome. He was not satisfied with the sentence, and on January 13, 1897, a stay of proceedings was granted in the

Supreme Court, but not by Downen's efforts; he did not care. All he wished for was the end, one way or another.

He was doomed to durance or death, and he preferred the latter. The case then came up in the Crimnal Court, and he was convicted to the penitentiary at Canon City, Colorado, for life. Shortly after arriving there he escaped, but was recaptured. He jumped on a horse that one of the officers had left standing just inside the prison gate and boldly rode out and away. He was dressed in stripes and must have been an impressive looking rider. He was not missed for some time, and they caught him just the other side of Florence, Colorado.

Six months ago he wrote a letter to Chief Russell, asking him to come up and see him. With his natural impulse of sympathy, the chief temporarily forgot his stallion and immediately responded to the summons.

Downen asked the chief to assist him in getting a pardon from the penitentiary. He asked him to write a letter to the President recommending the pardon of Downen. Chief Russell told the convict that he would never suggest or indorse such a thing, because he was too dangerous a man to be at large. Chief Russell told him, though, that he would assist him in anything that would benefit him or the public without injuring either.

Unless Downen escapes in some mysterious way, he will serve his life at Canon City, where the fortress of the Rocky Mountains shelters the gray walls of justice, shelters the reliquary of human woe, where freedom is forfeited in recompense for crime; but Thomas J. Tynan is the famous "big-hearted" warden there, and he has transformed it from a place of despair and degradation to a school where the lifers are pensioned and contented, and the others have the opportunity to rise to great intelligence, and when they face the world (liberated) each one is proficient in his or her special profession—that is the diploma that Tynan gives his graduates. He has changed the gloomy sullenness of their visages into visible joyous ambition. In Downen's own words, "All we lack is freedom, and that is the sweetest thing in life."

Since Tom Tynan has become warden he has imparted his irresistible optimism, and the prison has taken on the aspect of a fortified palace. With kindness and sympathy and singular understanding of human impulse, he has regenerated each convict into a man or a woman whom the world will need, and moral mastery is the vital power he has specialized, and they realize that each day they spend in the care of this big-hearted warden makes them better fitted for freedom.

He has turned their crimes into achievements for the state. Through them he has accomplished a scenic wonder of infinite beauty, linking a silent, haunted wilderness with the glamour and mirth of the land of skyscrapers, a wilderness haunted with traditions of the "happy hunting ground" and the dead of the red race, whose bodies were buried in the feathery arms of the great ragged pines which still guard the human bones that time and growth have vaulted in their mammoth trunks.

Warden Tynan has "beat the aeroplanes to it" by constructing an eight-mile highway along the crest of the famous Royal Gorge and thereby made it possible to joy-ride up into that inspiring wilderness in the modern touring car and touch nature in its wildest form from your seat in the throbbing machine. The smooth, hard road glides in and out of ravines in amazing evenness, forming a magical union of the modern and primitive with the steady rise upward to where you taste the clouds and scent the sacred mystery of that virgin wilderness.

A dash along the crest of the Royal Gorge is
a dash almost off into the rainbow that dips down
the canyon.  Then you get out of the car and creep
to the very edge, fearfully looking down thousands of feet to where the Denver and Rio Grande
tracks look like a rope and the birds a little ways
down look like flies.  There, way in the bottom, is
the famous Hanging Bridge, a miniature play-
thing from that vantage.

The blue clouds and purple shadows move below you and war for possession of the canyon.

This highway is a trophy of Warden Tynan's
administration. It was formally opened in the summer of 1911, and the dare and ardor of early days
was evident in the ceremony.  When the prairie
schooners tracked their way around the canyon
walls, little did they signify that the then unknown automobile would dash madly up to that
appalling heighth; little did the pioneers know
what an eden they were opening to the world,
and little did the convicts know when they committed their virulent crimes that they were the
machinery ordained to make Tynan's original
dream a reality.  Governor Shafroth dedicated it
and in the name of Colorado expressed our pride
and gratitude to Warden Tynan.

Mirth and festivity united the free with the bonded in a fraternity of good fellowship.

Downen played in the prison band which struck up patriotic airs with a spirit that showed that the satisfaction of being useful inspired their lightheartedness, and their gala scarlet uniforms lent brilliance to the scene.

Colorado put on her "glad rags" and turned out in Western fashion, casting aside the fetters of the workaday world long enough to chant a ditty, join song with the convicts and clasp the hand of the warden with compliments for his scholars.

To joy-ride up there in the evening and live the enchanted night in that wonderland where the earth breaks through the windows of heaven, to see the grandeur of mountain moonshine with its wierd glow in the black canyon, where the foaming river drags its sparkling vesture, makes the mystery of the wild scene which savors of the days of "war paint" fascinatingly gruesome. Then, at dawn, the mountain sunrise makes the inception of day blush and light deposes darkness in the depths of the Grand Canyon as the Denver and Rio Grande Limited glides along in the bottom like a hissing serpent.

"Don't even waste crime, but reap a lustral harvest from it," is Warden Tynan's motto, for with free labor he has built this highway, which otherwise would have cost hundreds of thousands of dollars.

Nowhere else in the world offers such wild grandeur as this place in the gorgeous West, where the sheltering mountains open their arms to the weary toilers from out the land of sky-scrapers, where nature has seen its death.

What ambition and pride this generous warden has given his prisoners! Their motto is, "If I have sinned I have been useful to Colorado and have received a wonderful education of honor and resistence from Tom Tynan."

He has given them a work to be proud of when they are citizens. It is a monument to their victims, and so pleasant is their retribution that he has never had an armed guard over a convict camp, and has never needed one.

There Downen is today. Years have passed and he has grown older. In 1897 he wished for the end, and now, in 1911, the end is nearer at hand. Now he says he is glad he is living and hopes to some time gain a pardon. He shows plainly that he is master now of the criminal influence which dominated over his honor in the years of his "wild oats." "I will never commit crime again; there's nothing in it," he declares.

One look into his face gives you complete confidence, and you would single him out as an exceptionally trustworthy man from this impression. He is of the self-confident, dangerously fascinating type peculiar of Missouri, the type which charms you by its innate daring, the stock from which sprang Jesse James, who, though he appropriated lives and has a history blotted with blood, we cannot help admiring; and surely that admiration is unanimous, for when Jesse James, Jr., held up a train in Biue Cut, Senator James A. Reed, the famous prosecuting attorney, could not get a single juryman to convict a son of Jesse James.

Downen's diabolical smile is irresistible, and he has a lisping voice that gives you the impression of an untamed leopard's purring. He is intelligent and healthy, energetic and industrious, and manufactures paring knives at the prison.

His natural cleanliness speaks of his refined origin, and shows that he has never dissipated to any great extent.

He is a lover of flowers, and shows genuine

joy and pleasure at the least provocation, and is naturally humorous.

The heroine of his Bowery romance, Artie Dallas, now lies in an unmarked grave in the paupers' field, with only gray rocks to mark her resting place and only weeds to decorate it. No friend visits her lowly grave, but perhaps occasionally a wild bird hovers over the lonely spot, chanting a carol whose plaintive notes ascend into the infinite realms above and invocate "Be merciful to her, for she knew not what she did."

She had fiducially answered the call of death when quick consumption laid its fatal hold upon her dissipated body and she faded, rapidly and silently as a flower.

There, in a notorious resort in the underworld, she closed her eyes, her wild, startled black eyes that hopelessly flashed from out her flying dark hair.

It was all ended; Artie was gone. No more would she rove the streets bareheaded, with the winter wind pitilessly cutting her half-naked body, in a mad effort to find food and shelter; never again would she be found drunk in the Market street gutters; never again would Artie suffer.

She was altruistic and had never in her life hurt any one but herself.

God rewards such people as Artie Dallas for their sympathy and their sorrow, and His recompense to them is heaven.

Many an unalloyed girl in the vernal period of life who was waywardly balancing on the very brink of ruin she rescued.

"Go back to the home where love and respect is your dower, for you will never find it here."

"But Rosie Olson is a deity of lawlessness, and homage is lavished upon her," was the one answer for the lovely worldling with her wild-rose beauty, and radiance was a luring beacon to daughters of prominent families who craved the Bohemian freedom of a demi-mondaine.

"But Rosie Olson will some day be the disconsolate outcast of the very ones who court her now," was Artie Dallas' eternal answer.

"Then why are you here?" was the childish question always asked.

Over Artie Dallas' tragical face would come a brave, heartbroken smile that illuminated her wild eyes with a sacred, retrospective fire.

"Why?" her tremulous voice would vibrate with pathos.

"Oh, well, little girl, take care of yourself and follow the advice of one who speaks from experience when I beg you to turn back and claim your heritage of honor. Forget me," she would plead in her old, noble, sacrificing way.

General David Downen, a brother of the multi-murderer, is a wealthy and prominent cattleman of Pueblo, Colorado. He was general in the Union army of Colorado, and was, for a period, Commander of the Department of Colorado and Wyoming for the Grand Army. He won enviable distinction in both. When the record of his brother's crimes was brought to him he refused to believe it.

The gray-haired mother received it with brave agony, and soon after death relieved and rewarded her for her years of pain.

Why had this tender mother been doomed to helplessly witness such a career as her son Allen's? Out of a proud home where the word harmony expressed every passion, desire and act, he sprang like a virulent weed.

As a panther kills and devours the gentlest lamb with only his carnivorous instincts controlling him, so was murder an innate characteristic of Allen Hence Downen.

Whether this controlling part of his character was caused by horror of something that his mother may have experienced or heritage from some ancient ancestor, is not known, but it is certain that if an inheritance it came from far, far back and failed to affect his strong, sympathetic father cr his gentle mother, and also failed to affect his sisters or brothers, for General David Downen's honesty and trustworthiness has led him to a position in this world where he is loved and respected and honorably wealthy. Allen Hence Downn says himself that he is the only black sheep in the family.

Consider the picture of Downen in his stripes. Draw from the sullen defiance of his face some theory of why his life has been so remarkably brutal.

Study the anatomy of his head, measure from his eyes to the apex of his spine, from his mouth to that point. Do not these defective dimensions bear significance of something beyond our power of understanding?

From the pages of the Bible a popular phrase is drawn: "The sins of the father and the mother shall be visited upon the children, even unto the fourth and fifth generations."

It has been historically so and will be eternally so.

Did not Adam and Eve, who were the genesis of the human race, sin, and have not their sins been continually diffused throughout the following generations?

Therefore this child of kismet and atavism, Allen Hence Downen, is more to be pitied than condemned, for he could not master the intangible power that controlled him.

His passion for crime was master, his heart and soul were dormant, and only the most singular things and the love of that one woman, Artie Dallas, drew from them a betrayal of remorse and tender sympathy and evidence that he really was a human being.

The gapless chain of ancestral barbarity which takes the modern back to the primitive has, perhaps, so influenced his life that he was unable to deviate from the path that has led him to the penitentiary at Canon City, and is a human being who has only recently awakened to the realization, and when death claims his body and his heart and soul are taken before the Judge who sees all and understands the problems of life, whose complex figures are too intricate for us to comprehend, Allen Hence Downen will be understood.

He was a practically moral man, and never used his power over an innocent woman, choosing only the volunteers of the underworld.

Many have gone with the speeding years; many have followed their varying paths across the eternal hills of time.

Will Allen Hence Downen answer the next roll-call and will it find his soul incarcerated within the dim walls of requited crime or roving the wide world at random?

"Guilty of murder in the first degree, and sentenced for life."

It is well to remember some passages from Silver's book (see page 69, "Star of Blood"). It will be seen that the events seem to parallel Silver's life and her tragic end.

"The heroine of his Bowery romance, Artie Dallas now lies in an unmarked grave in the paupers' field, with only grey rocks to mark her resting place and only weeds to decorate it. No friend visits her lowly grave, but perhaps occasionally a wild bird hovers over the lonely spot, chanting a carol whose plaintive notes ascend into the infinite realms above and invocate, 'Be merciful to her, for she knew not what she did.'

"She had fiducially answered the call of death when quick consumption laid its fatal hold upon her dissipated body and she faded, rapidly and silently as a flower.

"There in a notorious resort in the underworld she closed her eyes, her wild, startled black eyes that hopelessly flashed from out her flying dark hair.

"It was all ended; Artie was gone. No more would she rove the streets bareheaded, with the winter wind pitilessly cutting her half-naked body, in a mad effort to find food and shelter; never again would she be found drunk in the Market street gutters; never again would Artie suffer."

(Page 72) "From the pages of the Bible a popular phrase is drawn: 'The sins of the father and mother shall be visited upon the children, even unto the fourth and fifth generations.' It has been historically so and will be eternally so. Did not Adam and Eve, who were the genesis of the human race, sin, and have not their sins been continually diffused throughout the following generations?"

This is another passage of significance. Were Silver's thoughts reflecting back to past deeds of her parents, and was she to suffer?

In Chicago Silver made many contacts trying to promote her novel.

Silver receives a letter of April 28, 1911 from Etta Klosky with A.C. McClurg and Co., Chicago. She read Silver's manuscript and informed her that it was not material for a book, but might be used for a magazine or newspaper.

Another letter from Etta Klosky, May 1, 1911. She suggests to Silver that she read another book in the McClurg publications which will give Silver an idea as to how to enlarge upon details and make it into a successful book.

**PUBLISHING DEPARTMENT**

## A. C. McCLURG & CO.

NEW YORK: 9084 METROPOLITAN LIFE BLDG.
SAN FRANCISCO: 746 PACIFIC BLDG.

**330-352 EAST OHIO STREET**

**CHICAGO**

April 28, 1911

Dear Miss Tabor:--

I took your MS. home with me last night, and rest assured that I finished it before retiring into the sacred sanctums of the night. Candidly speaking, the material is really not what would do for a book, although for magazine or newspaper articles it would do capitally. Now this is my own opinion, which of course may be altogether out of order, but just consider this outside of business, and I beg of you do not be offended . We hope to have Mr. Browne with us again the early part of next week -- and I can't wait to put my "two cents" in on your behalf. I trust this little "deal" may prove to be the beginning of long and pleasant relations between us -- do not consider this presumption, as indeed it is far from that. When I tell you that I am a Southern girl and left behind me "mid the green fields of Virginia," my chum, the sweetest girl in the world -- you will appreciate my feelings when I saw you come in. Indeed, you reminded me so much of her, that for the minute I was --well I don't know what I was -- but suffice it to say that I just "fell in love at first sight."

226

Now, I have intruded long enough upon your time, but
I hope to be forgiven. Nothing would please me more
than a line from you -- am I asking too much?    Do
you intend to be in Chicago for any lengthy stay? If
so, can we not arrange a time in the near future for
you to come up to my house? I'd dearly love to have
you come -- I've a sister at home and after speaking
of you last night, she urged me to have you come over.
You will pardon my incoherent ramblings, please, and
whatever comes of our efforts to get your book published -- as of course just because McClurg & Company may not find it suited to their particular line
of books doesn't mean that somebody else will perhaps not find it available -- remember that you have
the earnest wishes for success of at least one admirer
among the many that I'm sure you can proudly claim.
Again, as girl to girl, I ask your pardon if this
is in the least presumptious, and with cordial regards to both yourself and Mrs. Bondwell, I am.

                          Sincerely yours,

                          Etta Klasky

Would you drop a line to me at.
2251 North Avenue
                Chicago

227

PUBLISHING DEPARTMENT
# A. C. McCLURG & CO.
NEW YORK: 9084 METROPOLITAN LIFE BLDG.
SAN FRANCISCO: 748 PACIFIC BLDG.
### 330-352 EAST OHIO STREET
### CHICAGO

May 1, 1911

Dear Miss Tabor:--

Again I thrust myself upon you -- but this time with a suggestion. Should you happen to be near our Retail Store (218-224 Wabash
Avenue) it would be well for you to go in and ask to see a copy of
"The War Maker," which you will find among the McClurg publications.
This, as you will see, is the life story of a very noted-- or rather,
notorious -- man. You will see how the author, Horace H. Smith, has
enlarged upon the details of the man's adventurous life. In fact, from
a little fact he has made a long, detailed, interesting account of many
wild escapades, daring ventures, etc. Now in case it should be suggested
could you do the same with your MS? It maybe that it is not at all
necessary, but as I have taken such an interest in the work, I'd like to
have you know all that is possible in this respect. You see the work
as it now stands, besides needing careful editing, is much too short
for any ordinary book. And if it should be issued by a general publishing house like A. C. McClurg & Company it needs must become "an ordinary
book" Don't misconstrue-- I mean "ordinary" in the sense of size and
manner of presentation, so that our regular travelling agents, etc.,
could handle it along with the rest of our line. Otherwise, the book
would have to be handled by special agents, and I'm pretty sure )from
knowledge obtained while in the Publishing Dept.) that McClurg's would
not care to undertake any such venture as this would naturally become,
were it an "outside" book. Now, please don't misunderstand my intentions.
I merely offer you the suggestion what it may be worth -- and I think you
will agree with me that no harm will be done if you take a look at this
"War Maker."

Mr. Browne is not at the office today, and he'll be so very busy
for the next few days to come, that I doubt the advisability of
trying to see him -- at least -- until say, Friday or Saturday.
As I told you, he would not be able to "pass" on the MS. for a
while at least -- until he had had time to see just what it com-
prises. (Strange workings of Fate -- your letter has just been

228

handed to me by the mail-boy). I note what you say regarding
the word "practically" and will submit the suggestion to Mr. Browne.
I'll "rub it in" that you have a tentative offer from Mr. Austin,
which you will accept if McClurg's render an adverse decision.
Oh, I hope we do publish it. I'm just as anxious as you are, and
"I'll do everything that I can to interest Mr. Browne in the work.
Does ""I will be very pleased to meet your sister" mean that you
will come to the house if I set a day? Yes? Well if your stay
here stretches into next week -- and if you can arrange it -- I
think Saturday afternoon will be just fine -- You see we are "off"
at one O'clock then and as I'm pretty busy in the evenings I can't
fix any other day. My sister is occupied so many evenings with her
vocal lessons, etc. (hacing to go out of the city three times a
week for them) that I have to wait until she can be home. Now
                    that
would be   all right for you? I hope so. If so, then I can tell
you definitely where to meet me -- and then I can take you right
home with me. "Don't dare tell me you can't say "yes."), for I'll
be more disappointed than I can say if I can't have you for a day.
Saturday afternoon I wrote to my chum (down in Va.) about you, and
she'll be anxious to know more about you, I know.   Oh, she's a dear
girl -- wish you two could meet each other.

        But to business -- I'm glad you do not take exception to
my letter -- and I trust you will receive this also in as good faith.
I'm going to count the hours until I hear the "momentous word that
will bring us two together again"-- (sounds like a novel-- but I
really mean it,anyhow).

        I thank you for having let me read the,work and rest
assured that I will respect your confidence -- but you may also
rest assured that you have one at this end who has your best interests at heart -- and I will do all I possibly can for you.

        Thanks for indulging me this long -- and let me know
whether Saturday May 13 will be all right -- By the way,let us
consider that date a good omen-- shall we not?
                        Sincerely yours,

Silver continued her struggle to become a successful writer, using whatever contacts she had. W.B. Griffin of the Cleveland *Leader* offered some encouragement. Blanche, to whom he refers, was the wife of Philip McCourt (Silver's Uncle). Blanche had previously been married to Mr. Griffin.

*NEWSPAPER FEATURE SERVICE CO.*
*Leader Building*
*Cleveland*

*Aug. 1, 1911*

*My dear Miss Tabor: A bundle of letters from Chicago reached me here today and among them was your welcome note and the card from Blanche. I have been on the Cleveland Leader for about three weeks, after I had taken a trip to New York. Had intended to return west after seeing Gay Gotham, but received a good offer here and like the town and the work very well.*

*It certainly was a relief to hear from Blanche. Shortly before I left Chicago a man from Denver came through who said he heard that she was dying of consumption and had to leave Anaconda. Evidently that was a mistake or she would not be planning a trip to New York. I will appreciate it deeply if you will let me know how she is and what you hear from her.*

*I surely did see the story and picture of you in the Journal. Fred Lawrence was very peevish at himself because he had overlooked such a good feature. I have since seen the story and picture reproduced in a dozen different papers.*

*How are you progressing in your literary work? Please let me hear from you often and it is possible I may be able to place some of your work here.*

*Yours sincerely, W.B. Griffin*
*Editorial Dept. Cleveland Leader*

Silver was interviewed by a Chicago newspaper reporter. She was quoted as follows: "Money is the God of Chicago. Manhood and womanhood and character are all that counts in the mountains. Chicagoans look sad. They do not know what the buoyancy of right living means. I don't care for the attentions of men, least of all Chicago men. Give me my pony and wild dash down the mountain trail. Give me the freedom to do and dare close to nature, and as nature bids. Chicago

230

disgusts me. Bright lights, music, revelry have no charm for me. I hear the call of the mining camp, and I want to go home."

Silver was homesick, and wired her Uncle Peter for money to return home.

Silver did not find a publisher for her book in Chicago, and returned to Denver. Here the book was also rejected. Silver was disappointed and discouraged.

Baby Doe came to the rescue, and somehow got the money together to have the book printed. Silver had very little money, and Baby Doe used her small income from the Matchless.

A Denver printer did the job, and hoped to make a profit since the name Tabor, he felt, should make it a good seller. Some Denver papers ran notices of her book. The Denver *Post* carried a review and picture of Silver. Stores in Denver stocked a few copies. Curiosity prompted some Denverites to purchase the book since it was written by Silver Tabor. A few hundred copies were sent to Chicago and sold. Silver supplied every literary editor in Chicago with a copy.

In another letter of September 13, 1911, Mr. Griffin advises that his paper, The Cleveland *Leader*, will use Silver's story and perhaps her verses:

*THE*
*CLEVELAND*
*LEADER*                    Cleveland, Sept. 13, 1911
*Dear Silver: You must think me an ungrateful person for not writing sooner and acknowledging the receipt of the papers, your letters and stories. The Sunday editor has been on a month's vacation and mapped out the papers in advance, so I have been waiting for him to return to see about your story. We are going to use it, if not in the Sunday section on the editorial page. Both the managing editor and Sunday editor complimented it very highly.*

*I dont know whether you would care to come east or not, but I think I could get you a position here if you cared to come. I really was surprised at the excellence of your story* [letter illegible here] *your verses are quite remarkable. You undoubtedly are going to be a great success as a writer. Cleveland is a very nice city and think you would like it here. There are three women on the staff now, one a society editor, another a club editor and quite a talented young woman who writes sob and special stuff. She has just returned from Richmond, VA., where she covered the Beattie case for us. I am head of the copy desk here.*

*I certainly was glad to hear that Blanche was not ill and that she is getting along so well. I hope she is happy, because when we were married I didn't appreciate her and made her very unhappy. This has always been on my conscience and I suppose it always will be. However, I am beginning to realize that supposedly broken hearts can be restored. I have an offer from the New York World I am considering and may go down there next month. Let me hear from you soon and would like to hear if Blanche has gone East.*

*Yours sincerely, William B. Griffin. Regards to Mr. Ward & Gene Taylor.*

William B. Griffin writes Silver again on February 10, 1912, advising that the Cleveland *Leader* did not use her story. She is disappointed that she cannot find a publisher for her convict story.

*Cleveland, February 10, 1912*

*My dear Silver: It was very nice of you to send me the little book, which I have just finished reading. I found it very interesting and original. Roy Giles, who used to be in Denver and is now on the Leader, is reading it now. Who wrote the review in the Post? I dont like the picture as well as the one that was printed in the Chicago Journal.*

*I shouldn't wonder if you are quite peevish over the convict story, but things have been torn up here and it was lost in the shuffle. I have been down to New York for the paper and returned only recently. The managing editor is in the Bermudas and I am taking his place. I found that the story had been killed in type along with a lot of Sunday paper filler and not even a proof of it remained. I found the cut in the morgue. If you have a copy of the story you might send it on and I trust it will meet with better luck next time. The paper has been all shot to pieces recently but if you want to come East I think I can fix it for you. Don Hanna, who owns the paper, decided it was losing too much money and there has been some very drastic retrenchment. I won out in the mix-up, though, and have a dandy job. I have had three promotions and raises in salary since I came here last July. Find that the world is much easier to get along with since I mounted the water wagon.*

*Write soon with some of the Denver journalistic gossip
and tell me all about yourself. I am sure you are going to
make a literary hit one of these days if you keep you your
work.*

*Sincerely your friend*
*William B. Griffin*

A letter to Silver from H.W. Conrad with the Colorado
Midland Railway Co. He thanks her for the copy of her book.

**THE COLORADO MIDLAND RAILWAY COMPANY**

GEO. W. VALLERY
PRESIDENT

OFFICE OF PRESIDENT
DENVER, COLORADO

IN YOUR REPLY PLEASE REFER TO
FILE

Denver, Colo., Feb. 12, 1912.

Miss Silver Dollar Tabor,
   Denver, Colorado.

My Dear Miss Tabor:-

   Allow me to thank you very much for the Autograph Copy

of the "Star of Blood," which you so kindly left at my office,

a few days ago. I left town the afternoon the book was left which

will account for my delay in acknowledging same.

   I will take very much pleasure in reading your work

which I understand is your first attempt.

   Again thanking you, I am

Very truly yours,

A letter to Silver from a newspaper friend, Jean C. Mowat,
in Stratford, Ontario, Canada. She writes that she has heard of
Silver's book away up in the north and east

233

*Stratford, Ontario, Canada*
*147 Dowers Street*
*February 12, 1912*

*My dear Miss Tabor:*

*Away up in the north and east I have heard of your great book,* **The Star of Blood** *and offer my sincere congratulations to you.*

*It has been a delightful pleasure to me to have met you and some day I hope it may be renewed.*

*There is a great blizzard raging to-day, & it is bitterly cold. It has been so cold that I have had both my feet frozen. At present I am serving in the capacities of—society editor, dramatic critic, book & magazine reviewer, rewrite man, copy-reader and assistant city editor in my spare time. My grandparents became lonesome & wrote to Chgo asking if I would not spend the winter with them & here I am. I almost went "dippy" with lonesomness, so had to go out and find some work to do. I may some day know enough to run a country newspaper.*

*I am glad, indeed, that you have made an impression on the literary world—keep it up. I am preparing to do it some time in the next five years. In the meantime I wish you success, & hope in the near future to be able to secure a copy of your book & have the pleasure of reading in entirety the story. From the review I judge it's a bully good story.*

*Remember me to Mr. Bliss if you see him, I expect to send him a reminder of Chgo newspaper days in a few weeks, in the shape of a short story.*

*Very sincerely yours*
*Jean C. Mowat*

## Chapter Nine

# *The Leaf in the Storm*

One day in Denver a very tragic event happened in Silver's life. Silver was on an errand for her mother which took her to a business man's office.

This man, behind locked doors, attacked Silver and chased her all around the room. Despite Silver's struggles she was seduced. Silver did not inform her mother about this terrible experience until five years later. Then she finally wrote her mother a letter, and explained that this man "threatened to kill us all if I told." Silver had a great fear of this man.

Silver was very high-spirited and Baby Doe was having difficulty keeping Silver under her control.

Baby Doe had visions of dangers surrounding Silver. She had always felt that devils would steal the Matchless from her, and now had visions of her dear Silver coming to a tragic end.

Silver was headstrong and very restless at times. She wished for something worthwhile in life. Surely, she thought, she would soon have an income from her writing. Not only did she wish to be self-supporting, but wanted to provide for her mother's needs also.

In 1914 Baby Doe and Silver were in Leadville. A bit of Silver's life is learned from a letter she has written to her mother. Baby Doe is concerned about the activities of her daughter and her friends. Silver has been living at the Vendome Hotel, but wants to leave there and move into a house. May and Josephine Fitzgerald are Silver's friends. Silver mentions Ted Brown who was also a friend of hers at one time.

Silver Dollar to her mother:

*Dear Mama:*

*I shall attend to your various matters to-day and tell you about them later.*

*As to the house—of course you know I **must** leave here or will have to, and that is the only place I know so if we do not go there I can not stay in Leadville because I have gone through every house and block in town and that was the only endurable place. And at the Hotel—you know so I can not stay here if some place just as comfortable does not turn up for I have to leave the Hotel.*

*And referring to Miss Miller spending the night with me—I can explain that if anyone is interested. As I told you I was going to—I started out to spend the evening with the Fitzgerald girls. May left us to go to the show—Josephine happened to pick up with her beaux Jim Fitzgerald and I went with Tom. I was not escorted by Ted Brown at all though I talked with him.*

*I will phone you later.*

*Silver*

Silver moved a number of times around Leadville. Baby Doe followed as closely as possible. She walked the streets of Leadville, at all hours, trying to keep her daughter from a life of sin. Baby Doe spent many sleepless nights worrying about Silver and her future.

Silver was unhappy and felt she was missing the good things of life. She remained away from her mother, and moved back to the Vendome Hotel for a time. (The Vendome was once the Tabor Grand. When the building was being constructed the owners ran out of funds. They asked Mr. Tabor for help, and he financed the completion. It was then known as the Tabor Grand Hotel.)

Now came a turn of events—Silver fell in love with a man named Ed. He and his friend Jim had arranged to lease the Matchless from Mrs. Tabor. Later Mrs. Tabor changed her mind about the lease, and would not let them have it. Mrs. Tabor did not want Silver to ever see Ed anymore. There was a long, bitter quarrel between Silver and her mother. Silver was broken-hearted, and felt life wasn't worth living. Baby Doe succeeded in breaking up the love affair.

Silver wrote her mother: "To whom it may concern, I Silver Tabor, this March 17, 1914 at 2:40 A.M. state that I am going insane or something else————"

April 20, 1914 Silver wrote to her mother that it was the end of everything. Ed stopped seeing Silver because he feared Baby Doe would cause trouble. Silver now intends to leave, and use another name. She does not want anyone to know where she is. She signs the letter—"The Leaf in the storm."

*VENDOME HOTEL*
*Leadville, Colorado, April 20, 1914*

*Mrs. Tabor:*

*Ed just came and said that we could not go together again. He is afraid of trouble from you. What did you tell him that I told you that he and I were going to get married for—when you know you were telling a lie and that I never told you so and why did you speak of the mask ball. You have no right to go into our personal affairs. He says he knows I never told you that we were going to get married. You have given me more sorrow than I ever expected to have. To-day when he said good-bye at the Hotel door I thought it was the end and now my heart is breaking. Under no condition show these letters or repeat one thing in them—that favor you **must** grant in the name of Jesus.*

*The end has come with me--life is a barren waste. And you gave me life.*

*I will not come up—never again—whatever you have to say to me write. Ed Levin of the switch engine will—I suppose—bring anything to me as he is in the hotel often.*

*Mr. Springhetti was in the lobby as Ed went this evening and according to my request Ed asked him what agreements he had from you regarding a Lease and Springhetti said he had no written agreement, which proved your lie.*

*The Mine will never do me any good in the years to come—I will be somewhere in another part of the world—apparently lost and you nor no one shall ever know where.*

*Ed has cut our going together off because he thinks you may make him trouble. I love him and would do anything to please him—even to living in the Cabin as he demanded. But it is too late—you have robbed me of him.*

*Of course you told him just what he said you did—I believe him—he has never lied and has been correct in all his statements. But you must not make trouble about it for he is lost and I will soon leave all behind me and face a gray future.*

*No one will ever be able to work that ground, I will always, no matter where I am, be ready and return to testify for him.*

*And above all things refrain from giving me more trouble during the few days I am here. No one but one person shall know my whereabouts and that person is not Ed nor anyone connected with him. How I am suffering.*

*I can borrow enough money to live on from a party here— not Ed nor anyone connected with him but from a man who has heard a lot of Charlies and [Ellis?] and Best's talk and who trusts and respects me. And then I must work somewhere but under another name and no one will know.*

*You should not have dared to mention anything to the expressman, it is no ones business and you have no right to peddle it.*

*No you do not love me—if you did you would not ruin my all—all is over. Ed does not know I love him and I never want him to know because he is lost.*

*May God pity you.*

*The Leaf in the storm.*

Silver writes another letter on April 20, 1914, continuing to vent her anger on her mother for breaking up the love affair with Ed. Again she signs the letter "The leaf in the storm."

*VENDOME HOTEL*
*Leadville, Colorado, April 20, 1914*

*Mrs. Tabor:*

*Ed told me that you threatened to disinherit me if I had anything more to do with him. And he is not going to have anything more to do with me—I knew that when he said good-bye at the hotel door and no one—not even my mother—is going to break my heart and manage to make the one I love desert me without paying for it so you are going to pay. You have accomplished what you have worked so hard to do—you have seperated us and given me a bleeding heart to carry on my desolate way—through my lonely life—a life without happiness or home life or love. So believe me—you shall pay.*

*You disinherit me and I will testify with proof so that you will have nothing to keep me out of. And you deed the things away and I shall put my proof in court and when you die if I am disinherited I will drag it through the courts and disgrace your name.*

238

LEADVILLE, COLORADO. April 30 1914

Mrs. Tabor:

Ed just came and and said that we could not go together again. He is afraid of trouble from you. What did you tell him that I told you that he and I were going to get married for — when you knew you were telling a lie and that I never told you so and why did you speak of the mask ball. You have no right to go into our personal affairs. He says he knows I never told you that we were going to get married. You have given me more sorrow than I ever

2

LEADVILLE, COLORADO_____ _____ 191___

expected to have. To-day
when he said good-bye
at the Hotel door I
thought it was the
end and now my
heart is breaking.
Under no condition
show these letters or
repeat one thing in
them - that favor you
must grant in the
sacred name of Jesus.
The end has come
with me - life is a
barren waste! And you
gave me life.
I will not come up-
ness again - whatever
you have to say to me
write. Ed Levin of the
Switch engine will - I

3

LEADVILLE, COLORADO.                    191__

suppose — bring anything to
me as he is in the hotel often.
Mr. Springhetti was
in the lobby as Ed
went this evening and
according to my request
Ed asked him what
agreements he had from
you regarding a Lease
and Springhetti said
he had no written
agreement which proved you lie.
The mine will never
do me any good in the
years to come — I will
be somewhere in another
part of the world —
apparently lost and
you nor no one shall
ever know where.
Ed has cut our going

LEADVILLE, COLORADO, _____ 191_

together of because he
thinks you may make
him trouble. I love him
and would do anything
to please him - even
to living in the Cabin
as he demanded. But
it is too late - you han
robbed me of him.

Of course you told
him just what he said
you did - I believe him -
he has never lied, and
has been correct in
all his statements.
But you must not
make trouble about it
for he is lost and I
will soon leave all behind
me and face a gray
future.

no one will ever be able to work that ground, I will always, no matter where I am, be ready and return to testify for him.

And above all things refrain from giving me more trouble during the few days I am here. No one but one person shall know my whereabouts and that person is not Ed nor anyone connected with him. How I am suffering. I can borrow enough money to leave on from a party here — not Ed nor anyone connected

with him but from a
man who has heard
a lot of Charlies and
Ellis and Bests Talk
and who trusts and
~~respects~~ respects me.
And then I must
work somewhere but
under another name
and no one will know.
You should not have
dared to mention
anything to the Express,
it is no ones business
and you have no
right to peddle it.
No you do not love me —
if you did you would
not ruin my life — all is
over. Ed does not know
I love him and I never

⌐

LEADVILLE, COLORADO,_____191___

want him to know
because he is lost.

May God pity you.

The leaf in the storm.

*When you ruin my life and break my heart and rob me of love—you shall pay. You will do nothing without my knowledge—that is beyond your power. And you shall also pay the price of not keeping your word, you said I could make them out tomorrow and then you refused. The laws of Heaven and earth say that you are not free to change your mind after a promise is made. And how dare you interfere in my love affairs. What would Papa say if he knew what you did to his Honeymaid. That lease belongs to Ed and Jim and if anyone else **ever** gets it they will put you in court and I swear to God—in the name of Jesus—that I will testify for them and how you told Ed and I that it was his only and how you told us all to-day that no one could have it but them and that it was theirs—so you see you have more on your hands than you planned. If you do not give it to them it shall never be worked until the end of time. And just think how willing they are to take it just the way you said.*

*I will never see you again by my efforts. I shall leave town soon but return to testify for the boys when they need me and all things you do in the business will be watched and told me and I may return for that. A woman, human and in love and having anticipated marriage and home and happiness will do all things for the one she loves—even if he has been torn from her—as he has. May God pity you in the other world for the crime you committed against your own child, a girl who is facing the world alone, carrying a bleeding heart, helpless to keep above in the storms of life and worst of all—**Alone** and robbed of **love** and **happiness** by her own mother—May God pity you when you face him in the other world.*

*I will not take your letters from the post office and all messages which come to me for you I will refuse to accept.*

*And if God does pity you and you ever see Papa—tell him that you sent his Honeymaid adrift in the world by having no pity for her and dragging love from her very hands, tell him that her frail figure is swaying in the storm, battered by the fires of life, that she is alone with a broken heart thinking of the happiness she almost had which you tore from her grasp. And tell him that I love my Papa and longed for his help and his protection.*

*And in the future when you wonder where and how I am—just think of me as "The leaf in the storm," suffering, battling for existance, alone and nursing the wounds of love.*

*May God Pity you.*

*The leaf in the storm*

[Added on next page of letter]

*Sharver and St. John must be paid.*

*Do not show this letter to anyone in the world—no one
must know about my broken heart.*

*Alone and helpless*

*The leaf in the storm*

*I did not pay Mrs. Newly. I needed the money for other
things—necessities—but I said I would try by the 25th, so
you can see that she gets $5.00.*

A letter to Mrs. H.A.W. Tabor (Baby Doe) in which Ed
promises to stop drinking. He wants Mrs. Tabor's friendship
and the lease on the Matchless. He is broken hearted about the
end of his love affair with Silver.

*THE HOTEL LAW*

*Eighteenth and Stout Streets*

*Just Opposite New Postoffice*

*Denver, Colo., May 6th, 1913*

*Mrs. HAW. Tabor*

*I do not know what to say, my heart is broken. I made an
ass out of myself and friends, but said nothing rong at your
hotel I asure you. And I never before was rong with you in
any way. Now at 6:10 I was fine and within ten feet of the
door of the hotel, had drank milk with R.G. Mullen my
friend all afternoon. And he was so proud as he is my
friend all the time. And is willing to advance me some
money on the prospects of the futer. As it may be, now. I will
ask you to come up tonight and at least call Mrs. Noland
up. Poor dear her heart is broke. I wish I was with Stephen,
and if the poor boy could see how I feel he would sure pitty
me I know. You know all and I am at your mercy as a
friend. I never reniged in my life and dear Silver she must
be disgusted with me I know, but if she had one hundred
friends like me she would be President of this U.S. I hope
you will apreciate my humiliation and ans. I can get this
money and all I want is your friendship and I positively
refuse to drink with anyone from now on, but get poor sick
momie some money. Poor dear is I am afraid going into
consumption. Please ans.*

*Ed.*

247

## The Hotel Law

### EIGHTEENTH AND STOUT STREETS
JUST OPPOSITE NEW POSTOFFICE

Denver, Colo., May 6th 1913

Mrs H A W Tabor

I do not know
what to say, My heart is
broke I made an Ass
out of myself, and friends
but said nothing rong
at your hotel. I assure
you. And I never before
was rong with you in
any way Now at 6½ I was
fine and within ten
feet of the door of the
hotel, had drank milk
with R G Mullin my
friend all afternoon.
And he was so proud.
as he is my friend
all the time. And is
willing to advance me
some money, on the

June 1, 1914, Silver is still broken-hearted and writes her mother to protest losing Ed and all future happiness.

Silver's Uncle Pete continues to send her money. On December 29, 1913 he sent a draft for $50.00 and said "glad Phil is with you and hope that you all have a very very Merry Christmas." Uncle Pete, May 2, 1914: "Enclosed find your May check. I am glad you like your pony, but hope he won't hurt you. With lots of love, Uncle Pete."

February 18, 1914: "Enclosed find Wells Fargo Express check as per your request to Mr. Spencer. I am very glad to send you this, and will send you a like amount on the first of each month—With lots of love, Uncle Pete." His stationery was headed:

Broadway Theater
Silver Circuit
Peter McCourt, Manager
Denver, Colorado

June 13, 1914. Silver writes Harrison Dewar. She has had a short love affair with him, and wants to know if he is still interested. If not, she asks to be released from all promises and to accept the attentions of others.

*VENDOME HOTEL*
*Leadville, Colorado* [June 13, 1914]

*Dear Harrison:*

*I feel that we should have a clearer understanding in order that I may know what to do. I made an agreement with you and am ready to keep it with pleasure if you keep your part of it. But I do not feel that I should be bound to reject all pleasures while you go free enjoying yourself apart from me.*

*I am anxious for the agreement to be kept by us both and so far I have kept to my part. Of course it was made before the tricks of jealousy and treachery had added the finishing touches to the storm but in this storm which has temporarily dimmed the clear, bright light of respectability I do not feel equal to standing entirely alone and carrying out your instructions to prove the falseness of all the charges without your assistance and comradeship which I counted upon when we planned.*

*You will understand my position as a girl—that I can not afford to reject the company of others if you do not intend to keep to your part.*

249

*I wanted you to phone me so I could arrange with you to talk this over. I expect to spend the night in our new dwelling place—221 E. 10th and oh, I am so anxious to be keeping house again.*

*I am able to hold my head up now in the same old way for all the citizens are greeting me with the same effervescing warmth and keen respect which assures me that they do not believe what they hear because of my past record of purity.*

*Will you let me know just how you stand in this matter and if you stand by my side come to see me at once and if not tell me that I am free to accept the attentions of others.*

*And no matter what to-day may hold or may not hold—I hope that all the years of our lives will at least hold a warm friendship.*

*Very sincerely,*
*Silver [Nutlets?]*

*June 13, 1914*

A letter to Baby Doe from Silver June 1914: At the top of the letter is a notation written by Baby Doe which says: "Received this last night—Sunday, or rather this morning 6:30 A.M." Silver's letter reads:

*It is now 6:30 A.M. I have stayed up unable to sleep—all through the night thinking of what you said. And through the long, quiet hours alone in my room I have come to the horrible realization of my lot in life. When a woman reaches 23 she should gaze back upon a differently trodden road from mine. Pleasure should have walked with her on that road, riding should have filled the days, dances and theatres the lonesome nights, young company should have thronged it. I gaze back upon a desolate road in which pleasure never ventured, upon which I walked apart and neglected by the pleasure feasting people of the world. My childhood was shadowed by sorrow and poverty, in girlhood I walked warily along my lonesome way, shabbily dressed and unhappy. And then I became a woman, the only improvement in my life being better clothes—but still alone. You must realize that you are incapable of supplying in yourself the thrills of gayety and young company whch is necessary to a girl my age. And now I stand gazing ahead upon a road as bleak and hopeless as the trodden path behind me which holds twenty three weary years. Tonight you told me horrible things about the person who has stepped out of my life and whose presence left a*

Dear Harrison:

I feel that we should have a clearer understanding in order that I may know what to do. I made an agreement with you and am ready to keep it with pleasure if you keep your part of it. But I do not feel that I should be bound to reject all pleasures while you go free enjoying yourself apart from me.

I am anxious for the agreement to be kept by us both and so far I have kept to my part. Of course it was made before the tricks of jealousy and treachery had added the finishing touches to the

*faint glimmer in my past gloom and whose absence brings
a stinging pain. I have taken terrible oaths to satisfy you,
telling Jesus Christ to kill me that instant in agony if I
knew of any possibility of me marrying him. Even those
strings did not satisfy your morbid desire to know more.
All I ask for this person is the respect of silence because that
part of my life in which he played the leading part is tender
to me, it is the one part of my life which I wish to have
respected without the sordid airing that the persecuting
things you say give it. Only my lingering thought and my
flooding tears must tenderly enter that silence wherein that
which should have ripened faded and in which is buried
that mission in life for which God created woman and
filled her with fiery impulse and longing that she should be
fitted to play her part. And not satisfied with the fact that
all through the long, still, silent hours of night I weep as I
dream of what would have been only for you—of what has
left my life forever and left anguish in its wake—you tell me
tonight that the reason you stay out nights is to spy on him
and find out and prove all the terrible things on him for my
sake and because of the agony I endured in the realization
of it all—would it not be possible to let him rest in the past
with the only happiness I ever had in life—happiness for
less than three months. And if it is not possible one of us
must leave Leadville, otherwise I would go insane. The
strain has been agonizing and now that the faint perfume of
the past is being overwhelmed by the stench of your constant
increasing spying—it is positively unendurable. I am
willing to let the rest of my life be absorbed in the fray but I
am not willing that the sacred romance of my life be
desecrated by your monarchy. If you are willing to close the
door on him and the past he played in my life so that I alone
can tenderly enter that past to dream and weep—then I can
live on here. I give you this letter to give you time to decide
what you will do before you decide about the house. And
what you do now must be binding and not temporary and if
you do as I ask it must be permanent for I think that my
broken heart is agony enough without your constant
torment and the realization that you are viciously spying
on the one person who is sacred to me and who is now out of
my life—do you think I would be suffering such agony if
this were not the truth, and every day my suffering grows
more intense as I watch the gap widen to an unbridgeable
distance. Carefully consider and then decide for good and*

*truthfully—tell me your intentions that is all I ask from you.*

Silver

*For Papa's sake, as I am his child please realize that I am a human being. Robbed of the essential parts of life and turned into a machine to please you—I am a mere possession over which you have ownership.*

*P.S. And with it all you solemnly kneel before God in prayer, telling yourself that you are justified in robbing a human being of the most essential things in life and causing overwhelming agony in order that your mighty will may be obeyed—in order that your parental authority and owner- ship may not totter on it's userping foundation but I say that you have no right to ruin my life and trample on the sacred tenderness of the only happiness I have ever had. Of course the maturity and realization of that happiness are forever impossible now and the least that you could honorably do now would be to refrain from trampling on the memories and the grave of that dead joy.*

*P.S. You will also have to agree not to go out hunting information about him and not to ask questions about him and to silently let him melt into the past. And you will have to promise not to slur him to anyone or talk bad about him.*

September 4, 1914. Silver writes her mother after a fracas at her boarding house the night before. Mrs. Tabor unex- pectedly burst in on the party in her daughter's room. The guests made sudden departures in all directions. In the confusion, as they fled from the house, Silver fell and injured her shoulder and side. Silver is furious about being humiliated in front of her friends.

Silver is still heartbroken about losing the man she loves and wants nothing more to do with her mother.

*Mother: Under **no** condition will I have anything more to do with you. I tried it again with Harrison Dewar and Jimmie Gildea but it has been a **damn** failure. There was positively no excuse for last night. The only way you could have honorably done anything would have been to wait until they left—then you could have given me hell. There was no excuse because we were commiting no crimes—just sitting there having a friendly lunch and chat. I will **not** come to see you nor admit you to my apartment and if you come here I shall ask the Walpenskys to keep you out. I hope* *you have not made me lose my home here—I have not seen them yet—God knows what I will do if I have. Send me an answer to this tonight by someone else—not you. I wish no more from you—if I can not find a job I shall starve. Please make arrangements for someone else to get your mail—not mine. And I insist upon you sending me my revolver at once and a letter to Turner stating that I can have things in the warehouse at any time. This must be an irrevocable order. What ever you decide to do now must be for all time and you must be bound by it and not change your mind at any time. You knew the low ebb of my heart last night and you didn't care just so you could carry on your mastery. All through the night I thought I was surely breathing my last from the excitement. You have given me this heart trouble by cruelly and knowingly taking the man I worshiped from me—I am positively dying from it and can never recover. I am not strong like I used to be—I am not really able to work with my broken heart but you have forced it. God—He alone knows what you have done by taking Ed from me.* [part of letter missing] *to get away from you because I haven't the money and you know that. There are two ways open to me to protect myself—my heart—and keep my home here. The essence of them both is having nothing to do with you— keeping you out of my affairs and from minding my business or making trouble with my friends and **away from** this building. One course is for you to make up your mind to do so and swear to do so and at the time when you should fail I will then take up the other course which is to use the hand of the law to keep you at bay. No one can charge me with wrong as I am doing now—I am 23 and have proven it and **you are not going to drive me out of my home and out** of this town if I can help it. If you are not willing to be subdued the law will make you. You know what you have done to me about Ed and Father Guida knows it for I wrote him in detail to ask prayers for my agony and his intercession with your heart of stone. And the world believes in me now and they're going to continue and you're going to stop raising hell. That fellow jumped last night in an impulse of foolishness and I seriously injured my shoulder and side by falling last night when I fled from the house. I must have an answer—if not I shall seek the law's protection. His name is Smith and I can prove it.*

*Your daughter.*

*Please don't give me any excitement to-day for I am so low with heart failure that I can hardly get around the house and cannot leave it. I would sink in the street.*
[September 4, 1914]

September 14, 1914. Baby Doe, in desperation at Silver's leaving her, sent a night lettergram to her brother Peter McCourt:

*The Postal Telegraph-Cable Company*
*NIGHT LETTERGRAM*

*Mr. Peter McCourt*
*Opera House, Denver, Colo.*
*Call her up tell her to come Denver at once bring Horse all her things. She will tell you she come back for things. Say no don't take no. She promised to go with me for few days trick. Make her bring all. Life or death—you must protect her. I shall never leave her. She must not know I have sent this letter. That you have again heard from me. You don't know where I am. Fail not. I am her Mother. Help for her sake poor child.*

*Lizzie*

Peter wrote Baby Doe (he always called her Lizzie) that if Silver wanted to get married and the man is respectable to not object. It was the natural thing to do. He writes that Silver had written him bewailing the way she had been treated by her mother.                    Sept. 15, 1914.

Dear Lizzie:

I received your telegram last night and immediately wired you. If Silver wants to get married and the man is respectable I can't see any objection. On the contrary it is the natural thing to do. I got a long letter from her the other day bewailing the way you had treated her. In this letter she stated that she was going to Colo. Springs to try to get a position and promised to write me from there. If I don't hear from her by tomorrow I will get some one to locate her and have her telephone me and will let you know the result.

Your brothe.,
Pete

Notte: _____ ____ condition ___
) ____ anything more to do
with you. I tried it again
for Harrison Dewar and Jimmie
Gilden but it has been a dam—
failure. There was positively
no excuse for last night.
The only way you could have
honorably done anything ___
___ been to wait until
they left — then you could
have given me hell. There was
no excuse because we were
committing no crimes — just
sitting there having a friendly
lunch and chat. I will not
come to see you nor admit
you to my apartment and
if you come here I shall
ask the _____ to keep
____. I ___ you have

Sept. 18, 1914.

Dear Silver:

      Was pleased to receive your two letters. I am very glad that you have left Leadville and hope you will get good and strong.

      Am sure you will enjoy your pony, which I am glad you have with you. Your mother informed me in her telegram that you had given it away.

      I think you are making a mistake in not letting your mother or any one else know that I am helping you financially, not on my account, but on your own, because the public always wonders where a person without a visible income gets his or her money. By letting people know that I am helping you people will think all the more of you, especially as you are a girl.

      There is no necessity of your coming to Denver for a few days. Jess and I may go down to Colo. Springs next week, and if so we can have a little talk about your future. In case I don't go down I may have you come up here to spend a few days with us. What do they charge you for your board and room? I wish you would write me a letter every few days as I want to keep in touch with you.

                  With love,

                      Uncle Pete

Miss S. D. Tabor,

    318 North Tejon St.,

        Colo. Springs, Colo.

Mr. Peter M-Court—
          Opera House Denver Colo

Call her up till her to come Denver at
once bring Horse all her things she
will tell you she come back for things
Say no dont take no She promised
to go with me few days trick
make her bring all, Life or death—you
must protect her I shall never leave
her She must not know I have sent
this letter that you have again heard from
                                        me

You dont know where I am fail
not I am her mother help for
her sake poor child
                            Lizzie

New Year's, January 1, 1915 found Silver writing from Colorado Springs to her mother. She addressed her Mrs. Phillips Room 20, Milo Hotel, 19th and Broadway in Denver.

She accused her mother of making her suffer hunger and has nothing to eat. She writes that her Uncle Pete offered her fifty dollars a month to live with Claudia ($25.00 for board and $25.00 to Silver). Or another alternative would be that he offered Silver fifty dollars a month to live with her mother.

Silver had been getting fifty dollars a month from her Uncle Pete anyway, and now did not like this new arrangement. Baby Doe had gone to Denver and talked over Silver's future with him, and they decided Silver must be with her mother or Claudia and not flitting around the country getting into trouble. Silver had quit her work with the Film Company, and had not been able to get a position elsewhere. Again Silver reminds her mother that she prevented Silver's marriage to the man she loves. She wrote her mother, "As his wife now, I would not be starving, I would be in his home and happy." She had now pawned all her best clothes for food and had nothing left. In closing her letter she wrote, "May God forgive you for the agony and starvation you have caused your child."

September 10, 1914. Silver has letter from her mother with ten dollars to save Silver's piano.

> *My Darling Child Silver:*
> *I send you this Ten dollars. Don't let any one take your Piano. I will fix it all O.K.*
> > *Your loving*
> > *Mamma*
> *Sept- 10- 1914*
> *We have found the holes-big-(3) in water pipe as I told them they would.*

My Darling Child Selmer;

I send you with this ten dollars $10.00 —
Don't let any one take your
Piano — I will get it all O.K.

Your loving
Mamma

Sept – 10 – 1914

We have found the holes (3) in water
pipe as I told them — they would

260

## Chapter Ten
# With Stars in Her Eyes

November 8, 1914. Silver writes her mother about her work as a movie actress.

*THE PIKE'S PEAK FILMS COMPANY*
*Office and Studio*
*610 N. Cascade Ave.          Colorado Springs, Colorado*
*Dear Mother:*
   *I received a night letter this morning and am very very sorry that you are sick. Write and tell me what is the matter. I am writing this at the studio, I am all made up ready for work but the sun is poor to-day and I do not think we can make any pictures.*
   *I am going to move into a private house, where they keep a few roomers, a very refined, strict place. I am going there as I can have the barn and keep Polly for about six dollars a month by feeding her just hay and alfalfa and no oats and not having her shod and not riding her. I can turn her out in the back yard in the day time and do the work myself. I will need the revolver so if I have to go way out to the barn on dark nights, if I heard noises there, I wouldn't be so terrified. Polly might get sick or something. She is sweeter all the time. Don't send me any money—you need that yourself and I would die if you did without anything to send it to me and I know how you need it. I can get along if I can have my coat and revolver. I am washing and cleaning and making all my old clothes over. I am made up as a spinster to-day but I generally have pretty parts. However it makes me more desirable for I can take any part. I really have made good and done perfect work from the very start. It will fortify me for my long, lonesome life and I don't have so much time to brood and be unhappy, I'm always busy or tired. Write me right away. I do not believe you want to lower yourself by writing to me yourself.*
                    *With love, Silver*

Silver returns to Denver and stays for awhile at the Pierce Hotel (13th and California Streets). She writes her mother that she is moving from the hotel, disgraced when Baby Doe paid her rent and left three dollars at the desk, making the comment that Silver needed it for food.

Silver remarked in her letter that she could not get another nice place for the price she had at the Pierce and would "have to live in a joint."

Baby Doe always gave whatever she had to help her daughter, but Silver remained resentful.

She seemed destined to failure, becoming discouraged when her attempts at newspaper work, poetry, music, or her novel all came to naught.

Silver finally joined The Minstrel Maid Company in Denver as a chorus girl. A short time after her first appearance, Phil Fredericks of Lakeside Park came to see her, offering her $100 to make a slide for life by her teeth at Lakeside. Silver accepted the proposition and writes to her mother of the unfortunate escapade that forced Silver to flee from Colorado.

*Chicago, Sept. 27, 1915*

*Dear Mother:*

*I received your letter just before I left Denver. I hope I shall never have to be seen again by anyone who knows me and if I ever pass through Colorado with a Show I shall be so well disguised—and use another name—that no one will recognize me. I left Denver with the Minstrel Maid Company as a chorus girl. Harry Hart was producer. He is the lame man you knew at the Milo who told you all about the penitentiary. He is a brute to work for, always drunk and a vile temper. I quit four times, before the company went on the rocks, and each time went to work again to please Shane and Anderson, the owners. They would have made good if Hart hadn't done them out of a lot of money and played dirt at every turn. Shane and Anderson were fine men. When the ship was about to sink Hart blew out unexpectedly.*

*He is the lowest cur I've ever met. When I left Denver Phil told me that anytime I got up against it to wire him so I wired for enough money to come to Chicago. Work is plentiful here but I am having a hard time to get a place as I have not had enough chorus experience. I think I can manage to get in some company 'tho.*

262

CHARLES T. LOWNDES
President

OTIS B. THAYER
General Manager and Producer

J. F. UNDERWOOD
Secretary and Treasurer

## THE PIKE'S PEAK FILMS COMPANY
### (INCORPORATED)

OFFICE AND STUDIO
810 N. Cascade Ave.

Colorado Springs, Colorado

Dear Molter:

I received a night letter, this
morning, and am very very sorry
that you are sick. Write and tell
me what is the matter. I am
writing this at the studio, I am
all made up ready for work but
the sun is poor to-day and I
do not think we can make any
pictures.

I am going to move into a
private house, where they keep a
few roomers, a very refined, strict
place. I am going there as I can
have the barn and keep Polly
for about six dollars a month by
feeding her just hay and alfalfa
and no oats and not having
her shod and not riding her. I
can turn her out in the back yard

Tom.

in the day time and do the work my-
self. I will need the revolver so if
I have to go way out to the barn
on dark nights, if I heard noise
there, I wouldn't be so terrified.
Polly might get sick or something.
She is sweeter all the time. Don't
send me any money—you need
that yourself and I would
die if you did without anything
to send it to me and I know
how you need it. I can get along
if I can burn my coat and
revolver. I am washing and
cleaning and making all my
old clothes over. I am made up
as a spinster to-day but I generally
have pretty parts. However it
makes me more desirable for I
can take any part. I really have
made good and done perfect
work from the very start. It will
fortify me for my long, lonesome
life and I don't have so much
time to brood and be unhappy,
am always busy or tired. Write me
right away. I do not believe you want
to harm yourself by writing to me yourself

When I was working for the Lambert Shows in Colo. farm towns, I learned an egyptian dance. That helped out some for Saturday night I got the job of dancing for a little social. They paid me Five Dollars and it saved me for Saturday morning my last cent had gone. Hart used to tell the bunch, about every day, that he saved you from starvation all last winter by going out and begging or stealing money or food for you. He is a beast.

A few days after I joined the show in Denver and while we were rehearsing Mr. Phil Fredericks of Lakeside Park through Sam Gates, a high wire walker who I met with the Lambert show and to whom I said that I would be willing to make slides for life by my teeth or feet—offered me One Hundred Dollars to slide by my feet on a wire from the tower at Lakeside into the Lake where two men would catch me. Gates sent Cameron and his carpenter Farran to arrange with me for Labor day. I was broke and accepted the proposition. A very green, common girl who called herself Florence Wheeler joined the show. She put up a pitiful story to us all of being a poor, innocent girl with no relations. She couldn't do a thing in the theatrical line but we all fell for her and the Co. kept her out of charity. She didn't have any clothes so I gave her an old hat, a white duck skirt and a middle.

This evening Cameron and Farran came to see me about the slide and just after they came Florence Wheeler came in and she was drunk. I told her I was talking business and to please go to the parlor until we were through. I was not having a party. I had never seen the men before but I knew Fredericks and Gates who sent them. She said she'd go to the parlor but had to go into my bathroom first. When she came out she said, "Some one of you three have stolen my 1/5th of a karet white sapphire ring." I said, "No Florence—it must have fallen off and we will find it." As I tried to soothe her she unexpectedly hit me in the eye and it temporarily blinded me. I almost fainted and my eye was closed. The men grabbed her as she tried to hit me again and then she started to scream. The neighbors called the police. Plain clothes men came in a big open auto and we were all taken to the City Hall. There I and the men were searched and my real name given as the detective got it from the Hotel. We were locked up pending investigation. I asked the matron to get me some beef steak or something for my eye but she said she couldn't be bothered. Early in the morning the detectives came and took me to my room to look

*for the ring and it wasn't to be found. When I returned
Florence was up and dressed and she said to me: "Silver,
I'm so sorry I gave you all that trouble but I was drunk. I
found my ring for I remembered having pinned it under
my skirt with a safety pin while I was in your bath room.
I'll have the case dropped but I don't want the police to know
I found it for it will make me look foolish." I told her that if
she didn't tell them I'd have her searched so she told it all to
the matron and detectives. They tore into her and scolded
her until she was hysterical and she said to me that if she
didn't get to go when I did she would kill me when she did
get out. Of course they turned us free without a trial. The
news wouldn't print it or the times or the Express and I
phoned the Denver Post that morning and begged them not
to but they said they would anyway. So I was fully
disgraced. I moved up by the rehearsal hall, to the Hoovey
and did not go on the street while I was in Denver. I went
and said good-bye to Phil and Blanche one night after
Twelve o'clock. Blanche told me that Fanny Borstadt's
mother who lives at the convent told about Florence being
put out of there after she had stolen money and clothes and
everything she could lay her hands on. Then a few days
before she got me in trouble she lowered her suitcase on a
rope out of the window at the Page Hotel and the rope broke
and they heard it and put her in jail and Harry Hart got
her out. He knew all the time what she was and helped her
fool the rest and put a thief in our midst. He took her out
with the show against the demands of Shane and Anderson
to leave her, and she couldn't do a thing on the stage. When
we were in Sterling, Colo. he had to let her go because the
Police told him she was wanted in St. Louis on stealing and
white-slave charges.*

*I'm tired of this life and if I ever have money to live on so
I won't have to support myself I'll do nothing but writing. I
have not been to see Claudia and am not going. If I don't get
a job I'll be starving when the Two Dollars I have is gone. I
had to give the hotel Two Dollars and that left me three.*

*When you write to me address me: Miss Ruth Knight,
Genl. Del. Chicago. I use that name now, no one knows me
here. What is the news about everything and everybody?
Write me all you know.*

*Claudia just got out of the Hospital, so Blanche writes
and Tilden is living with her now and has a broken arm.*

*I will close as I'm very tired, walked my legs off to-day
trying to get work.*

267

*I hope you are well, etc.*
                              *Lovingly,*
                              *Silver*


Ollie Underwood, a Denver friend of Baby Doe's, wrote to her in Leadville, informing her of Silver's activities in Denver. Silver and Ollie were staying at the same hotel.

*8/27/15*

*Dear Tabor.*
   *Your dear letter reached me a day or two ago. There is no use telling you how glad I was to hear from you for you already know. And you also know dearie it comes from the bottom of my heart when I say it too. "Silver" left here a day or two after I wrote you last. The chamber maid didnt know that I knew her (Now don't feel hurt at my telling you all.) She used to speak of her to me as that show girl in Room 115. I said one day what show girl, what is her name. She said it was Tabor. Then she said she was going to leave town with some Co. and was making a white costume trimmed in gold to wear on the stage. Then she told me* **some horrible** *looking fellow came up here to see her one night and she told her it was an old friend also that her mother hated him. And then she was supposed to leave town. But Billy tells me she met him on the street and she said she was living at the Bellvedere with some girl. So thats all I know about her.*
   *"Brother" sends you his best. He is getting along fine and is going back to work again, in fact he went fishing last Sunday of course he is not real strong yet. He still has housekeeping on the brain but not for mine.*
   *I have lots tell you that I can't put in writing. In case my letters go astray. I went to step off the car the other day, slipped in the mud and sprained my ankle. So cannot walk without a bandage on it and is quite painful.*
   *It certainly is a shame how you suffer from the fiends but that can't keep a good fellow down you know.*
   *We have had rain for almost a week. I mean every afternoon.*
   *Please write to me real soon as I love to hear from you and just address it here although we don't expect to be here much longer. I will keep you posted and let you know where*

*we are. Must say goodbye for now. With lots of love from brother. I remain.*

> *Your Sincere Friend*
> *Ollie Underwood*
> *"Tulu"     ha! ha!*

September 2, 1915. Ollie writes again and sends the newspaper clipping from the *Post* about Silver's being in jail. Ollie thinks Baby Doe should "try to come to her (Silver) or get her to come to you."

*Sept. 2- 15*

*Dear Tabor.*

*Please do not be angry with me for sending you this letter, for you know dear how much we both love you and I feel as near to you as one of my own family and I want you to take what I say in this light wont you. I hate to hurt you by doing it too, and on the other hand I don't consider I would be much of a friend if I didn't and I know you too well to think I do it with other than an interest I take in you because I love you.*

*I have heard lots lately that I have never mentioned to you in my letters just because I didn't want to make your good noble heart ache. But you know you can depend on me.*

*God bless you dear and may God give you strength to bear this new trouble added to the rest. I suppose you wouldn't believe me if I was to tell you I can hardly see for the tears in my eyes but it is because I understand and know your nature and heart so well. You will find this out sooner or later any way if you have not already and you might as well hear it from me.*

*This was in last night's "Post." I can not tell you how my heart aches for you and believe me those few who have talked of it to me got theirs for I tried in every way to defend Silver for your sake. However my object mainly in writing this is to ask you if you don't think you better try to come to her or get her to come to you. Poor child, I would go to see her and do anything I could but I was afraid she might tell me to mind my own business. If there is anything I can do for you let me know at once and know that my heart bleeds for you. Try to bear up under it and don't forget I am* **always**

*Your true friend in any way I can be.*

> *Ollie*

## HOTEL TIMMERMAN

MRS. LOUISE PETERS, Proprietor

**Running Hot and Cold Water in All Rooms
Rooms with Private Bath and
Telephone
Good Sample Rooms**

North Platte, Neb., _____191__

Chicago. Sept 27, 1915

Dear Mother:

I received your letter just before I left Denver. I hope I shall never have to be seen again by anyone who knows me and if I ever pass through Colorado with a show I shall be so well disguised and use another name that no one will recognize me. I left Denver with The Minstrel Maid Company as a chorus girl. Harry Hart was producer. He is the lame man you knew at the Milo who told you all about the

Another letter from Ollie September 11, 1915 relates how two people were discussing Silver's being in jail, and one said, "Oh well, her parents were pretty gay before her."

An interesting comment in Ollie's letter is that the cheap actress who caused Silver the trouble over the ring was putting on an act, and it was for the purpose of worrying Baby Doe.

*It will take you*
*all day to read this.*

*Sept. 11 -15*

*Dear Tabor.*

    *Your letter arrived yesterday afternoon and I certainly was glad to hear from you for I was awfully worried about you. I was beginning to imagine all kinds of things, in fact I was afraid something serious had happened to you and almost regreted sending that letter and clipping but I feel better now. Isn't it strange that I suspicioned that same thing after I got to thinking the whole proposition over. I came to the conclusion it was done for the purpose of worrying you. In the first place it seemed strange that that woman she got mixed up with there at that place should have been one of those cheap actresses. I wonder what she got for playing her part in that, evidently it was good pay for they say she acted it well.*

    *Do you suppose that cur you say she is married to is forcing the poor child to do wrong for him. It would be a snap for him for she is a beautiful girl. I wish she would let me be a friend to her but I know she wouldn't just because she knows I am a friend to you. Although I have never had any conversation with her about you. She doesn't know that I even hear from you as far as I know. I really believe that she moved away from here just because she saw me here. Poor foolish girl. If she only knew I would be her best friend if she would let me. If they wanted to spite and worry you it would have been enough, but they might have had principal enough in them to have spared Mr. Tabor's name. Poor man that is not here to defend himself and his. The vile wretches. There were two old hen (cats) got to discussing what they saw in the paper with Geo. and I one evening and one said, "Oh well, her parents were pretty gay before her." Say that was all that was needed for me. They seemed to think I was a **lady** before that, but I guess they think I am some hell cat now, and to h— with their opinion of me. After*

271

*I told one of them where to head in she said, "my dear you can't get away from facts." I said, Look here, what you look upon as **facts** I look upon as **damn lies**, and not only that if these were facts, and **I like** a person nothing you or any one else could say would change me.*

*Geo. had to try to cool me down. He said afterwards he was actually afraid I was going to throw something at her for I had gotten so damn mad I didn't know what I was saying or doing. She said, Well I certainly hope it wont make any difference in our friendship. I said, **we** never were friends, we were never anything but acquaintances and we will be less from now on. **There is no deceit in me.** They speak very cooly to Geo. now when they meet him & don't speak at all to me and I'm glad of it. The dirty low scum of the earth. I'll tell you Tabor I never went in much for this friendship business but when I do I am sincere in it. You will find that out. And some people hate me just because I won't be made a slave to the public opinion. I am who and what I am and I will do as I please and to h— with what they may think of me. And my skirts are cleaner than most of them at that.*

*I only hope and pray you will be in a position financially to ride on them some day. That is all you lack is the money. You are far above them now personally and I told that old cat so, too.*

*Don't you ever hear from Silver? I should think she could at least write you. She ought to remember you are **her mother** above anything else.*

*Don't expect to be here in this house very much longer. Am looking for something but sprained my ankle several weeks ago. And it is still very weak and has kept me from going out much. But just continue to send your mail here until I tell you not to. It will be alright. They are trying to get us to come back to "Milo" but he wont do it. By the way do you remember Mr. Gerhant who use to run that cooked food place on the corner of 18th & Glenarm and then moved over on to Welton street. Well you know he was in debt and after he closed up shop the other night, kissed his wife and baby goodnight, went into the kitchen of the store, made a pillow of towels on the gas range, put a towel over his face, turned on the gas and they found him dead the next morning. He was a nice fellow too. He was buried yesterday afternoon.*

*Am so sorry you are still having so much trouble up there. Brother says he is so sorry for you. I dont tell Unice*

272

*much you write me because she and Silver talk whenever they meet in the street.*

*Geo. is buying me a new coat for my birthday and must go down and have it fitted so will close now. Write me real soon as I will be worried if you dont. Do you ever hear from Dr. V— anymore haven't seen her but once since you left.*

*With love and best wishes*

*Ollie*

Sept 11. -15.

Dear Tabor.

Your letter arrived
yesterday afternoon, and
I certainly was glad to
hear from you for I
was awfully worried
about you. I was be-
ginning to imagine all
kinds of things. in fact
I was afraid something
serious had happened
to you. and almost
regreted sending that
letter. and stuff
but I feel better now.
Isn't it strange that
I suspected that
same thing after I got

274

to thinking the whole
proposition over. I came
to the conclusion it
was done for the purpose
of marrying you. in
the first place. it
seemed strange that
that woman she
got mixed up with
over there at that place
should have been one
of those cheap actresses
I wonder what she
got for playing her
part in _that_, evident-
ly it was good pay
for they say she
acted it well.
Do you suppose that
one you say she is
married to. is forcing

275

Mrs. H. H. Fulton
Leadville
Colo.

To
Public Libr.

INTERNATIONAL
DRY-FARMING
CONGRESS AND
EXPOSITION
DENVER
SEPT.27-OCT.9.1915

DENVER, COLO
SEP 3
1 30 PM
1915

276

## Chapter Eleven
# *Lovers and Liars*

Because of Silver's great fear of Stephenson, she keeps "on the move." She feels that joining the traveling shows gives her the opportunity of escape in one large city after another. She fears her life is in continual danger, and worries that harm will also come to her mother.

Circumstances were never revealed concerning Silver's marriage to Jack La Vode. It was a closely guarded secret. Not only does Silver flee from Stephenson, but tries to also escape the clutches of the criminal, Jack La Vode.

Leaving Denver, she tried to keep her whereabouts unknown. Her life style with shows only gets poor Silver into more trouble, and finally leads to her complete downfall and destruction. After being in jail, Silver was still so ashamed of this episode in her life that she felt she must surely leave Denver. In September of 1915 she left, never to return again. She joined the Minstrel Maid Review Company.

Silver's letters to her mother reveal that she had gone to Beatrice, Nebraska with a show that went broke and was stranded. Next, she went to Lincoln, Nebraska trying to find work as a chorus girl with the Beach show. This closed after a week.

April 5, 1916 Silver writes from Hotel Savoy Omaha, Nebraska.

Silver has an infected gland caused by blood poisoning she contracted in Indianapolis and is unable to work. She had a quarrel with the manager of the show and quit. All she has is 25¢, hotel bill, and a cat to feed. She writes, "I was born into a world of sorrow, nothing but suffering for me. No one to give me a little money to eat and pay rent with, I'm almost going crazy." Her trunk with her writings is being held for charges, her clothes are threadbare. "I've been a victim of circumstances, and now even my health is gone. And I'm cursed with an impediment in my speech which everyone makes fun of, and I have a tooth which never stops aching—which will cost fifteen dollars to have fixed. I guess there is no hope for me. Sometime the end will come, as it does to all shamed women who degrade themselves when driven on by hunger. I've been there many a time, with never a hand of help they go down and down to the end and a hopeless eternity when a lifting hand to feed them might have redeemed them."

Silver found cheap living quarters, usually on Chicago's old South side. Her pleas for money from her mother continue through the years. She lived under various names and changed her address often. Some of the names she used were: Ruth La Vode, Mrs. Norman, Mrs. Ryan, Ruth Reid, Ruth Knight, Rose Tabor, Mrs. R. Tabor, and R. Tabor.

*THE LINDELL*
*Lincoln, Neb., May 12, 1916*

*My Dear Dear Mother:*

*I rec'd your letter in Beatrice and was very glad to get it. The show had trouble there with the police. Beatrice is a strictly dry town but nine miles away is a wet town called Pickeral. The manager's son, the piano player, the ventriliquist and two chorus girls, Marie Russell and Margaret Harrington went to Pickeral one day in a Ford belonging to the father of two boys. The boys had the car and went along and got drunk. Because they were juveniles the police were wild and arrested our people but let them go on a fine. That same night the same bunch from our show, including the theatre manager, Mr. Higgins, and another chorus girl, Mary Dorcs, were arrested for drinking beer in their hotel and held in jail overnight. In Beatrice it is against the law to even drink beer. So the police gave the whole show six hours to get out of town. They did not all get away and those who did not are being held in jail. I was stopping at a different hotel and did not have money and I could not have gotten away only for the secret kindness of one of the policemen who rather liked me. He slipped me a ticket for Lincoln and I got away but had to leave my trunk* *for a $9.25 hotel bill. Now I am here without money to eat on. So I'm depending upon you to wire me some for I have only fifty cents left. The policeman had a dollar bill in the envelope with the ticket. It was good of him to get me out of town. This is a pretty fair town but when you are a total stranger you can't get help. However I am engaged for a stock Co. here which opens next Monday and I will get fifteen dollars a week. The manager was here in town last night and engaged me but he is gone now. I am feeling well. The weather here is very cool, too cool. How is it in Denver? Do not worry in the least about the cat. He is a wonderful animal and people now are going wild about him. He is so slick and beautiful and large for his age, five months. You know he was* [rest of letter missing]

She met a man by the name of Clair Sloniger. She makes up a great story telling him her mother in Denver is wealthy. Silver and Clair fall in love, and he later wants to go to Denver to meet her mother. Silver tried to prevent this. Clair had heard some bad reports about Silver, and wanted to check-up on her background. He also had heard that the Tabor lawyer, A.M. Stephenson, in Denver, had said that Silver had a husband in Denver by the name of Jack La Vode. Silver still denied this.

Silver, telling these lies to Clair, was now cornered. She was always very much afraid of Stephenson, and wanted to get away at once. She felt that when Clair returned from Denver, after his investigation, she could not face him. She feared Clair would surely find out she had been in jail in Denver. Silver wrote her mother asking her to write to Clair stating all this was untrue.

Silver had been ill, and had managed to get her uncle to pay for an operation. She had an ovary removed. Silver concealed most of the facts about her illness telling Clair she had treatment for female trouble and her appendix removed. June 19, 1917 Silver's Uncle Phil and wife Blanche inform Silver in their letter that they have sent $25.00 to the hospital, and $9.00 to the woman where Silver's things were stored.

On July 14, 1917, Silver, in Lincoln, writes her mother that Phil and Blanche will not send her another cent, but would send her a pass to Milwaukee so she could live with Lily until she gets well.

R. W. JOHNSTON
OWNER & PROP.

Lincoln, Neb. May 13 1916

My Dear Dear Mother:

I rec'd your letter
in Beatrice and was
very glad to get it.
The show had trouble
then with the police.
Beatrice is a strictly
dry town but nine
miles away is a wet
town, called Pickeral
The manager's son,
the piano player, the
ventriliquist and two

If only Silver had taken this advice and gone to live with Lily, her future life might have been much different.

### Destroy this letter

My Dear Mamma:

A.M. Stevenson is after me and I must leave here as soon as possible and go to some large place, probably St. Paul, and change my name again and live very quietly for awhile to protect myself. Now I will tell you the details. Over a year ago I came here from Beatrice, Neb., where the Schultal show was stranded. It was only a dollar fare and I heard that there were shows here which needed chorus girls but when I got here I was unable to get to work but stayed on promises to go to work at the Beach Show. That opened up and a week later closed but I stayed here awhile by getting money from you. When I was at the Beach theatre I met a young man whose people here are of high standing and wealthy. I went with him until the National Guards were sent to the Border and he wrote to me all the time from there and a couple of months after he returned I came to work for a show at the Lily here. I told him that I was from Denver and that my people were wealthy. I told him that you were wealthy. That was when I first knew him and just expected to have him as a passing acquaintance and as time went on and we became better friends I never contradicted what I had said but still said you were wealthy. Mamma, God alone knows how I have longed for a little home all my own so I could put the ups and downs of life behind me and have someone who cared for me to take care of me. And as he grew attached to me I dreamed of that. I told him I had never been married which is true. He often made the wish to meet you but I discouraged him going to Denver for fear he would hear that you were poor and about me having been in jail there and all that.

One week ago to-day he was out here to see me and made plans for a home for me and I thought that at last my dream was going to come true. He never came after that but this morning two friends were out and said that there were terrible reports about me around town. I at once knew what was the matter and feared that his people too might have heard and they have been lovely to me and strongly approved of me, so I feebly made my way down to the phone and called him up and told him I wanted to see him right away. He came out and told me that he was introduced to a man last Monday night who was from Denver and knew the

*Tabor lawyer—Stephenson and heard from him that I have a husband out in Denver by the name of Jack La Vode who is the notorious king of the Denver underworld and runs notorious resorts there. He told me to-day that he was not going to really take anyone's word for it but was going to Denver about the 15th of July to look up this Jack La Vode and also my people and find out the truth. La Vode is a name that I made up in my own mind but I told Clair that it was an old family name on your side of the family way back as you are partly French. I told Clair that I had never been married and could prove it and that I did not believe there was such a person as Jack La Vode. There are two things I know, one is that I must get away as soon as possible where Stephenson cannot locate me and that the other is that I must be away before Clair returns from Denver as I could not stand the shame of seeing him after he had heard about me being in jail in Denver.*

*Mamma, you are my only friend and I ask a favor of you. I told Clair that you were very religious and was so modest in your living that no one would know you were wealthy. If you see him or hear from him, for my sake please let him think you are wealthy and tell him that I have never been married and try to keep from him the fact that I was in jail there. He will probably find out though, for this man called me Silver Dollar Tabor and came direct with it from Stephenson. Maybe you could write to him and tell him that it is all a foul lie about Jack La Vode but please don't tell him that I said that I expected a home from him or any of that. I told him that I was going to write you all about the Jack La Vode lie so if you write and say that I wrote you and gave you Clair's name and said he was coming to Denver and to see you and that you thought you would drop him a line about it and not go into any details about anything except the lie about me being married and leave a wealthy impression it might keep him away from Denver as I cannot stand the idea of him finding out how unfortunate I have been. You are my only friend and take my advice about what to say as I am on the ground and know what is best in this case. They say here that I am a most remarkable patient to recover the way I have after all I had done to me. So as soon as I am able I must go away and be unknown and start in all over again. And I want you Mamma, to help me all you can in this disgrace. I shall stay in and be very quiet, both on account of my health and to keep out of Stephenson's way and with* your help and God's help I will get away and start again. Clair does not know that I had anything done in this operation except my appendix taken out and a little treatment for female trouble. He does not know that my ovarie was removed. If you write him tell him that it is a lie about Jack La Vode and that when he comes to Denver that you will be glad to see him and prove the lie for me. That will be a good stall. And use fair stationery and do not give any address as if you apparently forgot it. I know you will be my friend now and help me to get out and away with as little disgrace as possible. You are not supposed to know about me going away from here. You just know about Jack La Vode and Stephenson's plot. I told Clair to-day about Stephenson's treachery, how he had ruined me and also tried to beat you out of your money and properties. So stand by me now mamma and write him if you want to and write and tell me all you think about it. Address him—Mr. Clair E. Sloninger, Lincoln, Neb. and address me at 1734 N. St., as I will be leaving here tomorrow or Tuesday and may God help me to leave Lincoln soon. Clair said that one thing that made him believe it was because I had always discouraged him about going to see you and I said that was because I had not thought that you would approve of me getting married. Mamma, I rely upon you and God and God knows I need the help of both.

Your loving
Silver

*Lincoln,*
*July, 1•17*

*My Dear Mamma:*

A. M. Stimson is after me and I must leave here as soon as possible and go to some large place, probably St. Paul, and change my name again and live very quietly for awhile to protect myself

## Chapter Twelve
# All the World's a Stage

October 16, 1915. Silver's letter to her mother states that Silver, while in Chicago, went to Milwaukee, Wisconsin to see her sister Lily. Lily begged her to "blow the show," and stay there with her. Again, if only Silver had listened to Lily, how different Silver's future life might have been. Silver made an excuse for not accepting Lily's offer. It was, she said, because she was in debt to the show, and had to pay them before she could leave. She is tired of chorus work, and hopes to get work with a motion picture concern. She goes from Chicago to Indianapolis, Indiana and uses the name Ruth Knight.

October 14, 1915. Silver's letter from Indianapolis to her mother: Silver writes she is ill and has had another operation. She states she has had blood poisoning. She arrived with the Gay Widows Company, but had to quit because of the operation.

At the time Silver was working for the Lambert shows in Colorado farm towns, she learned an Egyptian dance. She continues to use this dance in later shows.

In this letter she mentions her dancing again and writes "there is some satisfaction in being a beautiful dancer and picked by a large audience as the prettiest girl in the chorus, and called to the front to sing." She mentions that this life has its drawbacks such as the recent almost fatal operation she just experienced. "I would like to go back to Leadville if I could work. I would fill my life with writing and music. There is more satisfaction in being a famous writer than an actress——I'd need a room to write and play in and a piano. My voice has improved very much."

She wrote she wouldn't mind living at the mine, but couldn't very well get along without running water in the house and a clean private room to work in. She wanted protection so she would not be afraid at night. She left trunks filled with her writings in Leadville. She used the name Ruth Knight.

October 15, 1915. Indianapolis, Indiana. Silver writes her mother that last spring she had to let Antlers Livery have her pony, Polly, for the bill she owed them. She still mourns the loss, and writes of her dreams about Polly. Her dreams are horrible and awaken her—they are about the pony coming to a terrible end. Name she uses is Ruth Knight c/o F. La Vode.

October 24, 1915. Indianapolis. Silver is not getting any more money from Phil, as he can't afford it. Peter refuses to send her any more money. Silver states she has had a serious relapse. Signed letter Ruth Knight.

Silver was pregnant. Her letters do not reveal the circumstances. It ended in a miscarriage followed by peritonitis and blood poisoning. Silver did not let her mother know about the miscarriage.

Silver had written her mother and told her that she had bladder trouble.

November 11, 1915. She continued to write her mother for money for bills she had to pay. States that she wants to go to Colorado, but does not promise. Silver says she is homesick. She mentions she has received a lovely letter from Lily.

January 13, 1916—Silver writes from Cleveland, Ohio to her mother: She is with the Big Review of 1916 Company playing a week at the Empire theater. She has been with this company for three weeks, but laid off to have an abscess lanced. Wants the news from home. Signed Ruth La Vode, Dixon's Big Review of 1916 Company. Burlesque Theater, Baltimore, Maryland.

January 28 from Harrisburg, Pennsylvania. Silver wrote her mother for help. She uses fictitious names as follows: "Dear Madam: Please try to locate Mrs. Maria Holzan that her married niece, who was ill last fall, is ill again and in Harrisburg hospital—she is to have an operation—Tell her to write Mrs. R. Wilkin surgical ward, Harrisburg Hospital. Truly, Ruth Knight."

Sick, broke, and out of work stranded in Lincoln. Silver wrote the Denver lawyer who had seduced her in 1912 and demanded money. He answered that she should come home to her mother. Silver, at this point, wrote her mother about the entire story of how this man seduced her.

Baby Doe, upset, answered, "Thank God you told me. Don't tell anyone else. He is a devil—be careful. Hide. He will try to harm you."

1915 November 15th to Mrs. Tabor. Letter from A.M. Stephenson of Denver stating he had a very pitiful letter written by Silver from Indianapolis, Indiana, saying she was just over an operation, and had been employed in a show as a chorus girl. "She asked me for a small amount of money, I did not reply to her letter, but put the money in an envelope, and sent it to her." He hoped the trouble between Mrs. Tabor and Silver would be fixed up "before it is too late."

In November 1915 Mrs. Tabor was very concerned about her daughter. She managed to scrape together enough money to make a trip to Indianapolis to investigate Silver's illness. Mrs. Tabor went to the office of Silver's doctor and asked him to inform her about Silver's trouble. After the doctor's explanation, Silver was confronted by her mother, now in an outrage. Silver was angry with her mother because she had gone to her doctor for information. A fight between the two followed which created an embarrassing scene.

After her mother's return home, Silver again kept writing for money. Her mother, filled with pity, sent money again. Always when contacted, her mother sent $10, $15, and even $30.

After the trip to see Silver in Indianapolis Baby Doe also went to see Lily. They are all upset about Silver. Silver moved from the Albert Hotel to Hotel Metropole. She had to leave her trunk for a $20 bill. She is canvassing from house to house for an embroidery firm. She says she is disgusted with show work. She needs $15 to get her tooth removed, asks Baby Doe to send her the money. Signs it Ruth La Vode.

Feb. 14, 1916. Silver writes from Hotel Hannah in Cleveland. Fills in her mother about being with the Big Review of 1916 when first taken ill. She was so sick she

287

couldn't pack her own grip. She was in such bad condition when they reached Harrisburg, Pennsylvania that she was sent to the hospital.

*THE HOTEL HANNAH*
*In the Heart of the Theatrical District*

*Cleveland, Feb. 14, '16*

*Dear Mother:*

    *I am writing this letter after having had no replies to my others. You may have very few more from me for the Doctor says I may never get well. I was out with the Big Review of 1916 when I was first taken ill. I had an abcess, on the exterior, caused by a bruise and I was trying to stand the pain and work. Finally it got so sore I couldnt and I had it lanced. The day before I had it lanced I had come unwell. The Doctor did not give me anything or put anything on it when he lanced it and I had a terrible faint. I suddenly stopped flowing and two nights later during performance I was stricken with violent pains and I had an engagement for a dinner party after the show. We went at once to the Hofbrau, a fashionable cafe here, and I drank two whiskies for the pain. Then I ate lobster salad and later on was taken so violently ill at my hotel that I thought I was going to die. All that night I laid screaming, high temperature and violent chills and violent pains in every inch of my body. The next day they had to pack my grip for me so I could go with the Co. For almost a week I was in that condition off and on and when we reached Harrisburg Pa., I was in such a serious condition that they sent me to the Harrisburg City Hospital where I laid in agony for three weeks. I wrote you a card from there and signed it R. Knight. I wrote on it that Maria Holzen's niece, who was sick last fall, was sick again and would like to hear from her Mother. If you do not write to me you will regret it for I think I am dying. The Doctor said to-day that he did not think I could get well. An anonymous letter came to the Harrisburg Hospital, mailed in that City, containing ten dollars, that is what I came here on. My temperature now is way below normal and I am sick, perhaps dying, without money or help. My feet are on the ground and I am in the greatest need so if you let me die, suffering, alone, in want without even answering my letter you will regret it to the end of your days. The Doctor says I must not work for awhile anyway while I try to get well but how can I eat or pay rent if I do not and I have to there is no chance of*

288

# THE HOTEL HANNAH

## 1122 SUPERIOR AVENUE, N. E.
### NEW NUMBER

### IN THE HEART OF THE THEATRICAL DISTRICT

**BELL PHONE, NORTH 521**

Cleveland  Feb. 14, 16

Dear Mother:

I am writing this letter after having had no replies to my others. You may have very few more from me for the doctor says I may never get well. I was out with the Big Review of 1916 when I was first taken ill. I had an abcess on the exterior, caused by a bruise and I was trying to stand the pain and work. Finally it got so sore I couldn't and I had it lanced. The day before I had it lanced I had come unwell. The doctor did not give me anything or put anything on it when he lanced it and I had a terrible

over

289

*recovery. I'll not try to hear from you again, if you will not
answer me now it will be too late.*

*Your child
Silver*

*Address:
Miss Ruth La Vode
Hotel Hannah
Cleveland, Ohio*

A letter postmarked Feb. 27, 1918 from Lily to Silver. Lily
writes, "wish I could ask you to come right up and see us, but
just at present we are terribly crowded. You know Uncle John
is here. We are looking for a larger flat."

Another letter postmarked Nov. 4, 1918 in Chicago. Silver is
using the name Ruth La Vode—writes she is broke and out of a
job. She complains about her poor clothes. She has been put
out of her room, and her possessions are being held for a $45
bill she owes the hotel.

*THE ANDERSON HOTELS*

*Chicago, Saturday*

*Dear Mamma:*

    *I cant understand why I don't hear from you. It seems as
if the end of the world has come for me. I know I cant hold
out many days more. I lost my job on account of my clothes.
My only dress and my shoes and coat and hat are so
dilapidated that they told me I'd have to have better and
neater clothes to hold the job. So I had to stop work to-day
and when I got home I was ordered to give up my room
because I couldn't pay the rent, and leave everything I had
behind, so now with 47 cents in my purse I'm going out and
all I can take is my comb and brush and toothbrush and
God alone knows what will become of me.*

    *Homeless and broke, I'll try to brave it out a few days
longer, hoping that I'll have another chance but God knows
how sorrowful and helpless I find tonight. I owe about
$45.00 forty five Dollars, hotel bills and everything I have
will go if I can't pay them, then if I don't get some new
clothes I won't be able to work for I am in rags now. I don't
mean fancy expensive clothes but just something neat and
that is not falling to pieces.*

    *Really I'm almost insane tonight and if God doesn't send
me help, I can't live much longer. I feel as if the end had
come and maybe it has. No one knows how I feel tonight.
May God give me strength to endure my suffering.*

290

# The ANDERSON HOTELS

W. E. ANDERSON, Prop.       H. C. STUART, Gen. Mgr.

TABOR MSS. COLLECTIO

I am stopping at
**THE MARION**

*Chicago,* Saturday

Dear Mamma;
I cant understand
why I don't hear from
you. It seems as
if the end of the
world has come for
me. I know I cant
hold out many days
more. I lost my job
on account of my

*I'm going out into the night now and I'll try to get a bed somewhere and for God's sake write to me anyway as my heart is breaking.*

> *Your loving child*
> *Silver*

In February, 1919, Silver writes from Chicago as Ruth La Vode and gives her address as c/o C. Buck, 646 East 41st Street.

She is still sick, and "I hope that I will sometime stop being sick." She never asks her mother for money again.

[February 28, 1919]

*Dear Mamma: I received your letter but have had an attack of pneumonia since and am just now able to be up and around. I hope that I will sometime stop being sick. It was absolutely necessary to cut into my jaw bone to prevent worse trouble as I had a terrible ulceration.*

*The picture is beautiful and I will carry it with me. I have not heard from Lily for a long time, she did not answer my last letter.*

*I have arranged for a place to receive my mail, so that I will be sure to get it. I do not live there but friends do. Address me—Miss Ruth La Vode, 646 East 41st St., Chicago, Ill. Care—C. Buck. I am going to have all my mail sent there so I will not lose any. You do not mention the business, please tell me about everything and about what you saw of Papa. It will be safe at that address. And take care of yourself and write me often.*

> *Your loving child*
> *Silver*

## Chapter Thirteen

# Silver Dollar— A Homeless Waif

In August 1919 Silver began to send her mother presents. Once a bathrobe and another time a box of lilies. Her stationery became better quality.

In a letter of September 16, 1920, Silver writes again from Chicago giving her address as 1635 Washington Boulevard. She addresses her mother at Leadville.

Silver asks her mother not to move up to the mine, but to stay at the hotel. Winter is coming, and if she needs help she can get it there.

She writes that two men friends are wild about her. She does not care for them. They are just ordinary men. Lily doesn't answer her letters. She has not seen Aunt Claudia. She talked to Ralph to ask about news of her mother. Aunt Emma died. Silver asks her mother if she received the picture she sent of Persis (daughter of Maxcy Tabor).

*Chicago*

*My dear Mamma:*

*I received your letter this afternoon, after I had mailed you one. I was certainly glad to get it, as I worry so when I do not hear from you. Mamma, please **don't** move up near the mine. Please stay at the Hotel, for winter is coming and it is so much better for you to be where it will be warm and where there is someone to see that you have help, if you need it. I won't send anything more to the Hotel. The reason I sent the lilies was so there would be no delay in the delivery. They were both expressed at the same time, so they should have come together. But I promise not to send anything to the Hotel again but please stay there where it is comfortable.*

*The little picture is lovely and I cried when I read your
letter and you told me about the visions and all. I often cry
when I think of dear Aunt Emma. She is so dear and sweet
to think about. There is a colored woman here in Chicago,
who is a very devout Roman Catholic and also a medium.
She told me that the sun would shine for me in the middle of
1921 and that all would be well for me and Mother then but
that until then we would still be struggling along. I believe
her, as she told me wonderful things. She described
Grandma and Aunt Emma and Uncle Stephen and also
Millard Page. She told me that we had found a man dead
in our home, years ago, and that he wanted her to tell me
that he had not died from epilepsy, as we thought he did, but
that someone had murdered him. She first described him
and then told me. She said that I was going to leave Chicago
and go first to Nebraska, then to Colorado, then to Salt
Lake City and then to California. She said that I would
probably get married and I told her that I never would.
And I thought so at that time but since then I have rather
changed my mind. I am still very undecided. There are two
fellows, both very lovely men but I do not care about either of
them, only in a friendly way, but they are wild about me.
They are both ordinary, that is I mean working men but
clean and refined. But there is no future for me with either
of them, only a home and living. The only reason that I
think of marrying is that I have been through such struggles
and I think that maybe I would be a little better off. She told
me that if I married, I would be terribly dissatisfied, and
that is the truth. But I believe her when she says that 1921
will bring a change for she was very emphatic about that
and she certainly described me dead.*

*I wrote a letter to Lily, quite a while ago but have received
no answer. Does she ever write to you? I have never seen
Aunt Claudia but Ralph told me, when I called up to see if
they knew anything about how you were, that they had given
up their home and were all living in a hotel. That was
terrible, after all her ranting and raving for a home of her
own. And she has every reason to be happy at home, for she
cares for Ralph and the children.*

*What did Aunt Emma die from?*

*And do you ever hear anything about Blanche & Phil or
Pete and his wife? I never hear anything so please tell me
the news. Did you receive the picture of Persis that I sent
you? Tell me all the news, as I never hear anything. Tell me*

*about the mine and the Maid of Erin and about the people I
know in Leadville and Denver.*

*Mama, please write to me more often, as I worry so if I
do not hear from you.*

Your loving child
Silver

*1635 Washington Bld.*

Silver corresponds with her mother at Leadville. Another
letter arrives from Chicago postmarked Nov. 10, 1920. Silver
is going to send her mother some pomegranates. She gives her
address as 4031 A Drexel Blvd.

*Chicago*

*My dear Mamma:*

*I received your letter some time ago and was relieved to
hear from you. I am going to send you some pomogranites
as they sell lots of them here. You peel them somewhat like
an orange by peeling the thin skin off but be careful of the
insides. Then you pull the sections apart and eat the
covering off the seeds but spit the seeds out after you have
sucked off the juice. I will send them by express as soon as I
hear from you. Well I must close for now and please
Mamma write to me as soon as you receive this.*

Your loving child
Silver

*4031A Drexel Blvd.*

Jan. 15, 1921, Silver writes, still in Chicago, and now at
Groveland Park Hotel. She has taken the name of Ruth Reid.

GROVELAND PARK HOTEL

[January 15, 1921]                                    *Chicago, Saturday*

*My Dear Mamma:*

*Just a line to tell you where I am. I have been ill and
could not write before. I am using a different name and will
tell you all about it later.*

*Please let me hear from you as soon as you receive this.*

Your loving child
Silver

*Address: Mrs. Ruth Reid*
*Groveland Park Hotel*

November 1921 another letter arrives from Silver, still at
the Groveland Park Hotel. She writes her mother she has been
in bed sick. Baby Doe is worried and wants her to come home,

but Silver writes she could not stand to make a trip for a while until she gets stronger. She continues, "there are many reasons why I could not come now, but I will come later when the Doctor says I am all right to go."

If only Silver would leave that life and go to her mother or accept help from her family.

GROVELAND PARK HOTEL

[November 5, 1921]

*My Dear Mamma:*

*I am writing this in bed, as I do not want you to worry about me. I am getting along all right but last Tuesday and Wednesday I thought that I was dying.*

*The Doctor says that I will be all right if I get rest and quiet and have no excitement for awhile and drink no coffee or tea or anything alcoholic. I never can drink coffee or tea again. Mamma Dear, I am all right and getting well but I must rest and be quiet and I could not stand to make a trip for awhile until I get much stronger. But do not worry about me as I am getting better and stronger day by day. Mamma Dear, there are many reasons why I could not come now but I will come later when the Doctor says I am all right to go. But for a while I must remain in my room and be very quiet, then I will constantly improve as I am improving now. I will write you more in a day or two and please don't worry as I will keep you informed about how I am getting along. All that I need is rest and quiet and no excitement and I am getting that here.*

*Please don't worry Dear, as I am coming along all right.*

*Your loving child*<br>*Silver*

*P.S. This is the first letter I have written myself so that shows that I am better.*

My Dear Mamma:

I am writing this in bed, as I do not want you to worry about me. I am getting along all right but last Tuesday and Wednesday I thought that I was dying.

The Doctor says that I will be all right if I get rest and quiet and have no excitement for a while and drink no coffee or tea or anything alcoholic. I never can drink coffee or tea again. Mamma dear, I am all right and getting well but I must rest and be quiet and I could not stand to make a trip

In a letter postmarked Feb. 18, 1922 from Chicago Silver writes her mother in Leadville. Silver is still at the Groveland Park Hotel and is not well. Writes about Aunt Tilly and Andrew. "Tilly looks great and Andrew is a model son." "Andrew promised me that he would see that I got a start in business. I am going to open up an exclusive little shop and then I can take care of you. It will be sometime this summer."

### GROVELAND PARK HOTEL
[Feb. 18, 1922]

My Dear Mamma:

I should have answered your letter long ago but I have had a terrible cold and wrenched my ankle, the one I sprained last summer, and I have not felt well at all.

Aunt Tilly and Andrew are here and they are both looking wonderfully. I have seen them several times. Aunt Tilly has the best of health and Andrew deserves a lot of credit as he is a model son. He has not married and has devoted his life to her. The three other children are married and all live in California and Andrew takes care of his mother. Every night he takes her to a show and they both seem very contented. Andrew promised me that he would see that I got a start in business. I am going to open up an exclusive little shop and then I can take care of you. It will be sometimes this summer and I will be very glad to be in business.

I received a letter from you, with clippings, one was about Father Pantanella and then one letter since then which I am answering now. I will close now and go to bed. Please answer soon and tell me how you are. I am going to have my last summer's coat cleaned and send it to you in a few weeks. It is a black satin dolman, a long one and you can get a lot of good out of it this summer around Leadville as it will cover up all your other clothes, and I used to go out lots of times with only an apron under it.

Well good-night mamma. Please answer soon.

Your loving child
Silver

Another letter from Silver to her mother is from Hotel Carleon, 2138 South Wabash Ave., Chicago. She writes how she lived in the Groveland Park Hotel for over a year. She says she was sick most of the time and still owes them about $70.

298

They are holding Silver's trunks for the bill. She still mentions Andrew setting her up in business.

[April 22, 1922]

*HOTEL CARLEON*

Chicago

*My Dear Mamma:*

*I was so glad to receive your letter as I worry when I do not hear from you.*

*I lived in the Groveland Park Hotel for over a year, and I had nothing but sorrow, all the time I was there. I was laid up for over two months with a sprained ankle, and I had that terrible spell of enlargement of the heart and two attacks of the flu and then pneumonia. I still owe them about $70.00 and they are holding my things for it. I am glad I moved for I have new hope now and perhaps I will have better luck. Some places are voodoos and that Hotel certainly must be one of them. I am only here temporarily as a friend of mine is taking a ten room flat the first of May and I am going to room and board with her. She is a fine girl and I have known her a long time and besides being cheaper it will be home to me. I am going to have my satin dolman cleaned and send it to you but I have to wait until I get my trunks as it is packed in one of them and I will send it as soon as I can. I am glad you had those lovely dreams about me, maybe they mean that things will change for me. I certainly hope so as I want to be able to help you. Andrew promised to set me up in business and if he does so, everything should turn out all right but of course all he did was promise. Please write me soon. Your loving child*

Silver

R. Reid
2138 Wabash Ave.
Chicago, Ill.

Oct. 19, 1922 Silver writes using the name Ruth Reid and the address given is Hotel Huntington, 37th and Langley, Apt. 106.

Nov. 9, 1922 Silver writes of her plans to work in a florist shop that a friend will open.

*November 9 -1922*

*My Dear Mamma:*

*I received your beautiful letter and the picture of St. Anthony.*

My dear Mamma;

I was so glad to receive your letter as I worry when I do not hear from you.

I lived in the Groveland Park Hotel, for over a year, and I had nothing but sorrow, all the time I was there. I was laid up for over two months, with a sprained ankle, and I had that terrible spell, enlargement of the heart and two attacks of the flu and then pneumonia. I still owe them about $70.00 and they are holding my things for it. I am glad I should for I have new hope now and perhaps I will

300

*I let some of my friends read the letter and they said that
I must have a wonderful mother. I only wish I could help
you along and I am hoping and praying that some day I
can.*

*The weather has turned very cold here and I hate to see
winter come.*

*A friend of mine is going to open a Florist Shop and give
me charge of the shop and I will love that for you know how
I always loved fern in the window, and I get more pleasure
out of that than anything around me. They have a lot of cats
and kittens in the Hotel and they all come calling on me
and that is another thing I enjoy.*

*Mamma dear, please write often, as I worry about you.*

*Your loving child*
*Silver*

Silver writes on Christmas 1922. It is a lonely Christmas.
She hopes to be with her mother next Christmas. Uses the
name Reid, Hotel Huntington, 37th and Langley, Chicago.

*Christmas*

*My Dear Mamma:*

*This is a lonely Christmas for me. It always is for I think
of home and the snows of Colorado.*

*It is very warm to-day. Few people are wearing their
heavy coats and that seems so strange to me.*

*Next Christmas I hope and pray that we are together.
Maybe you will come here to live with me and I am going to
make an effort to go to Colorado for a short visit this
spring.*

*Mamma dear, always remember that you are the nearest
and dearest thing in my life and that if God will help me,
we will be together this coming 1923.*

*Your loving*
*Silver*

*Reid*
*Hotel Huntington*
*37th & Langley*
*Chicago, Ill*

A letter from Silver at Grant Park Hotel in Chicago, letting
her mother know her latest address. She philosophizes: "It's a
hard pull, isn't it? I wonder if things will ever be easier?
Perhaps things might be different, if I could be different."

Christmas

My Dear Mamma:
This is a lonely
Christmas, for me, but as
always is one's thought
of home and the
snows of Colorado.

It is very warm
to-day. Few people
are wearing their
heavy coats and that
makes it strange to
me.

Next Christmas I
hope and pray that
we are together. Perhaps
you will come here
to live with me

GRANT PARK HOTEL
*1148-1150 Michigan Blvd.*
*My Dear Mamma:*
*I want to let you know my new address. The apartment house, where I lived, at 3802 Grand Blvd., was sold to colored people. They started to move in and of course all the white people moved out. I only expect to stay here for a short while, as I want to find a place where I can cook. I am staying temporarily, with a girl friend.*

*I received your dear letter and should have answered sooner. We still have Winter and that is very unusual. Last year this time, I didn't even wear a coat and to-day was almost a blizzard.*

*Why don't you ever tell me the news from the old hometown, all about who dies and marries and leaves. I would so enjoy the news.*

*Also why don't you ever tell me about yourself. How you are and how you are getting along. It's a hard pull, isn't it? I wonder if things will ever be easier. Perhaps things might be different if I could be different. I'm so afraid to wander away from the legitimate path. I'm afraid of the danger and the price that people pay for breaking the law. I guess it is your prayers that give me the fear to keep me back. Sometime we may all be rewarded for our struggles. Mamma Dear, please answer soon.*

*Your loving child*
*Silver*

*Ruth Reid, care—Mrs. McHale*

In another letter postmarked May 15, 1923, Silver uses the name Ruth Reid, care of Mrs. R.T. Hill, 417 North Clark street. "Saw Aunt Tilly and Andrew but I don't see them anymore. Aunt Tilly was sweet and Andrew was very good to her, but he tried to start something with me. . . ."

[May 15, 1923]
*My Dear Mamma:*
*I should have answered your letter sooner, but I was trying to get permanently located first. I have had a hard time to find a satisfactory place and have not yet succeeded. However I expect to stay here for awhile at least, until I can find nice, cool rooms for the hot weather. It is still cool here yet and the nights very cold. I never have seen such weather. Women are still wearing their fur coats. The hotels still have steam going and no window screens up yet. Why don't*

TEL. HARRISON { 6232
6233
PHONES IN ALL ROOMS

E. MILLER, PROP.

EUROPEAN PLAN
ELECTRIC LIGHTS
STEAM HEAT

# GRANT PARK HOTEL

### SPECIAL WEEKLY RATES
#### 1148-1150 MICHIGAN BLVD.
#### CHICAGO

My dear Mamma:

I want to let you know my new address. The apartment House, where I lived, at 3802 Grand Blvd, was sold to Colored people. They started to move in and of course all the white people moved out. I only expect to stay here for a short while, as I want to find a place where I can cook. I am staying temporarily, with a girl friend.

I received your dear letter and should have answered sooner, but still have Winter and that is very unusual. Last year this time, I didn't even wear a coat and to day was almost a blizzard. Why don't you ever tell me the news from the old home town, all

*you ever write me any of the news back home? I surely
would love to know what is going on back there, but I never
hear. Do you ever go to Denver? Do you ever hear from Phil
or Blanche? I suppose Claudia thinks it is funny that I
have never been to see her, after living in Chicago for so
long. You know I saw Aunt Tilly and Andrew, but I don't
see them any more. Aunt Tilly was sweet and Andrew very
good to her but he tried to start something with me and I
told him I never wanted to see him again and I never have.
Of course Aunt Tilly does not know anything about it. He
wanted me to make my home with them and all that but
what good would that do me with him trying to pull stuff
like he did. I'm awfully disgusted with all men. I've seen too
many of them. Please answer soon and let me know how you
are and tell me the news.*

*Your loving child*
*Silver*

*Ruth Reid*
*care—Mrs. R.T. Hill*
*417 North Clark St.*

October 11, 1923. Silver is now using the name Ruth La
Vode again and her address is the Drexel Hotel, 3958 Drexel
Blvd., Chicago.

She is very ill. Silver has been going with a doctor. "He has a
drug store and gave me all my medicine and whiskey." She
had been living on the West side but then moved south again.
She still thinks of Clair Sloniger in Lincoln whom she had once
hoped to marry.

[October 11, 1923]                                            *Saturday*
*My Dear Mamma:*

*I meant to write to you, at the time I sent the packages, but
I had so much on my mind. The woman I roomed with sold
the house and everyone had to move and all that goes to
make a person neglect things.*

*Since I moved I have been very ill and I am just now
recovering. I had an attack of pneumonia and I was unable
to do anything. I have a friend here who is a Doctor. I go out
with him very often and if it had not been for him I might
not have pulled through. He has a drug store and he gave
me all my medicines and whiskey and was a great help to
me.*

*I was living on the West side on Washington Blvd. but
now I have moved out south again and I am staying at a*

305

small hotel until I can get located. I have to laugh every time I think of this hotel. They lock all the doors at one a.m. and if you are not in then, you have to wait until morning to get in. It is a fine place for owls like you and I. I am going out now to try and find a place to live. I am glad you liked the birthday gifts. I hope you ate all the candy and that you are wearing the bathrobe. You know it will be bad luck if you don't wear it for I bought it for you. I want you to wear it all the time and I will send you another for next winter. I wanted so bad to go West this fall but I could not get the money together. It costs so much to travel and money does not grow on trees. I hope I will get there sometime. Of course I will if I marry the fellow in California but I don't want to do that. I don't think I'll get married at all. I wanted Clair Sloniger in Lincoln but since I couldn't have him I don't want anybody. I wish I could forget about him but I cant. That is the burden we all have had to bear: "unhappiness."

Well Mamma I must close as I am running out of stationery. Address me here and my mail will be held and perfectly safe as they are more than honest and respectable in this hotel.

Your loving child
Silver

Ruth La Vode
Drexel Hotel
3958 Drexel Blvd.
Chicago

## Chapter Fourteen

# Ask Not for Whom the Wedding Bells Ring

Another letter to her mother. She writes that she is now Mrs. W.J. Ryan and that her address is 3706 Lake Park Ave., Apt. 11, Chicago. She married in August 1923 at the age of 33. "I have only a few more years before my good looks are gone." She continued, "I've planned all along on getting a rich man and paying up your mortgage and all our old bills in Colorado and all that, but I couldn't make the grade. God may help us sometime unexpectedly."

She refers to her husband: "He is good and will do anything in the world for me. He thinks first of me in everything— Mama dear do not worry about me anymore. I will be safe and will be taken care of. Sometime maybe you will come to live with me. We will talk it over if I make the trip this fall. And I want you to feel happy about me for I won't want for anything."

> *My Dear Mamma:*
> *Just a line.*
> *Did you receive my last letter, in which I told you about getting married.*
> *I gave it to a girl to mail and as I have not heard from you, I wonder if you received it. It worries me, as I do not like letters lost. Please let me know as soon as you receive this.*
> *I also moved, so it may have been lost through moving.*
> *Please answer right away.*
> > *Your loving child*
> > *Silver*

307

My dear Mamma:

Just a line.

Did you receive my last letter, in which I told you about getting married?

I _____ so to a girl I'm _____ and as I have not heard from _____, I wonder if you received it. I

*Mrs. W.J. Ryan*
*3706 Lake Park Ave.*
*Apt. 11*
*Chicago, Ill.*

Later, another letter arrived saying she had divorced Billy Ryan: "I guess you never know a person until you live with them. I am going to get married again this spring. And with this marriage will come prosperity and also a lovely fellow. He has a little girl and she is very sweet." Silver moved again, and gives another address—Mrs. Norman, 5044 Michigan Ave., 3rd Apt. "Put 'For Mrs. Ryan' on corner of envelope."

*My Dear Mamma:*
*Well, we are in the New Year and God alone knows what is in store for us.*
*Somehow I feel cheerful, so that may be an intuition anticipation, of the year ahead of us. I surely do hope so. I know you like me to write on plain paper, but this is all that I have and I want to get it off, so you will know my new address.*
*Mrs. Norman has taken a large apartment and it is extremely comfy so I think that this address will be permanent. We did not have snow until Christmas morning and then only a tiny bit. Then no more until New Years eve. Up until Dec. 31st the weather never got even cold but we are getting it now. And we will probably get it until about the first of May. I am divorced from Billy Ryan. I guess you never know a person until you live with them. I am going to get married again, this spring, and with this marriage will come prosperity and also a lovely fellow. He has a little girl and she is very sweet. Well Mamma, I must close and get this off. Please write to me very soon.*

*Your loving child*
*Silver*

*Address:*
*Mrs. Norman*
*5044 Michigan Ave. 3rd Apt.*
*Put: "For Mrs. Ryan" in the corner of envelope.*

Silver writes that she has moved again and is using the name Miss R. Tabor. She and a girl friend plan to open a dressmaking shop.

*My Dear Mamma:*

*I am just recovering from a fractured knee and that is why I have not written sooner.*

*I moved back to the South side, as a girl friend and I are going to open a dressmaking shop, for the better class of trade, and we expect to make good, in time.*

*We both know all about sewing and there are plenty of big shops here, which started on a small scale, and are flourishing now.*

*We can also make hats, to match dresses, if necessary and do all the fine and delicate work that the well-to-do women pay for.*

*Mamma Dear, please write to me and tell me all about everything. If we do well, in our shop, there will never be a week pass without you getting a money order. Of course it will take a little time to get going right, but in the long run it should pay well.*

*I was laid up, for several weeks, with my knee and am just beinning to walk again now.*

*Please write soon and tell me all about everything.*

*Your loving child*
*Silver*

*Address: Miss R. Tabor*
*3702 Lake Park Ave.*
*Apt. 8, Chicago, Ill.*

Another letter from Silver. She is moving to 1225 East 44th Place, Chicago, still using the name R. Tabor. She wants her mother to write.

*My Dear Mamma:*

*You will wonder why I have not written before, but I could not.*

*I got scalded, by steam, all over my face and chest and shoulder and hands and arms, and I was in bed, for quite a while. I planned on sending you a Xmas present but I could not do anything, but lay flat on my back. I have been up, for the last few days and I am feeling fine now. My face looks just the same and also my hands and arms. My chest was burned the worst and there are still red blotches on it, but there are no scars, and the Doctor says that the red blotches will disappear in a month or so.*

*I thought so much about you during the holidays and wished I could see you. I have a girl friend who was very good to me while I was in bed. She nursed me night and day as I did not want to go to the hospital. Her husband also helped me and lifted me up and down and he stayed up all night with me, part of the time. They really proved themselves to be real friends.*

*Mamma Dear, please write to me soon and let me know how you are. I think of you all the time. Please take care of yourself.*

> *Your loving child*
> *Silver*

*Address—*
*Miss R. Tabor*
*2109 Michigan Ave.*

Baby Doe, for years, had sent most of her money to Silver, but now she has no money. It is believed Silver was begging for this money to use for alcohol and dope. No wonder Baby Doe had little money to clothe and feed herself.

Chicago.
Jan. 18, '25

My dear Mamma:

You will wonder why
I have not written before,
but I could not.

I got scalded, by steam
all over my face and
chest and shoulders
and hands and arms
and I was in bed, for
quite a while; I planned
on sending you a line

## Chapter Fifteen
# *The End of a Silver Dream*

Silver at about 36 years of age came to a very tragic end. Newspapers carried the account of her death on Saturday, Sept. 18, 1925. She was then living at Apartment 23 at 3802 Ellis Avenue and had used the name of Ruth Norman.

The coroner listed her death as accidental caused by burns from scalding water and shock. Neighbors heard her screams and rushed into her apartment. They found Silver in agony suffering great pain. It is said she had spilled boiling water on herself. She had been heating water in a large kettle on a gas range.

The doctor said she was an alcoholic and a narcotics addict. Some years ago the author talked to the daughter of an intern working in Bethany Hospital in Chicago at the time of Silver's death. He said Silver had sclerosis of the liver. For several days there was no one there to claim her body. Silver's aunt living in Chicago identified the body at the morgue. Peter McCourt in Denver was notified and he sent $200-$300 for burial. Peter and Mrs. Tabor were horrified at Silver's fate. They read the glaring newspaper accounts containing the lurid stories of Silver's life and death. She was referred to as a soiled dove in Chicago's cheapest slums.

There was little that Baby Doe and Peter could do. They pitied Silver, but were ashamed of the disgrace brought to them and the Tabor name.

Baby Doe told reporters that the dead woman in Chicago was "an imposter." "My daughter, Silver," she said with dignity, "is in a convent."

Baby Doe always knew where her daughter was, and still had Silver's letter written August 4, 1925.

313

My dear Mamma;

Please write to me, as
I worry so, about you.
I have dreamed, of
you and Papa, so often
lately.

Please let me know
how you are.

your loving child,

Silver.

R. Tabor
3802 Ellis av,
apt. 23.

*My Dear Mama:*
*Please write me, as I worry so about you. I have dreamed*
*of you and Papa so often lately. Please let me know how you*
*are.*

> *Your loving child,*
> *Silver*

The return address on this letter was Rose Tabor, 3802 Ellis
Ave., Apt. 23, Chicago.

This was the last address of Silver Tabor.

The letters Silver has written all during 1925 do not indicate
that she has heard from her mother. Every letter Silver writes
asks her mother to write and let her know how she is. Not
having heard from her mother, Silver was becoming more
discouraged as the months went by. Baby Doe was broken-
hearted about Silver's life, and unable to do anything more to
help Silver. Baby Doe had tried in vain, many times, to get
Silver to leave Chicago and come to her. Silver never returned.

A picture was found in Silver's apartment. Silver had
written on the reverse side: "In case I am killed, arrest this
man for he will be directly or indirectly responsible for my
death." Because of this letter, suspicion surrounded her death,
and the man was held for investigation. He was later released
for lack of evidence.

This was not the first time Silver had been scalded. She
wrote her mother from 2901 Michigan Ave, Chicago, on
January 18, 1925: "I got scalded by steam all over my face and
chest and shoulders and hands and arms, and I was in bed for
quite a while." Signed Miss R. Tabor.

Silver was buried in Holy Sepulchre Cemetery.

Lily was about 18 years of age when she was allowed to
remain with her grandmother and Aunt Claudia in Wisconsin
and Chicago. After marrying she remained in the Chicago
area and never returned to Colorado. She still corresponded
with both her mother and Silver through the years. Silver and
her mother at various times visited Lily and other members of
the family.

After the death of Silver, newspapers carried the story that
Lily admitted her relationship, but stated she had not seen her
sister for years—"I wanted a quiet, decent, sheltered life. Why

315

should I who have pride and position and only like quiet and nice things have to claim her now in this kind of death?"

Silver had taken the wrong road, and her life had been miserable. When Lily and Silver were little girls, they had attended shows regularly in the Tabor Opera House in Denver until the loss of the Tabor fortune. Horace and Baby Doe were so proud of these little daughters as they danced "like little fairies" in the Tabor Box. They imitated what they saw on the stage, and often were the center of attraction as they frolicked about in the Tabor box during the stage productions. Now to think beautiful little Silver's life had come to such a terrible end.

In Silver's novel, *Star of Blood*, Silver had written about her heroine, "with only grey rocks to mark her resting place and only weeds to decorate it." Now Silver's own grave was alone with no marker. At last a stone was placed on her grave on September 18, 1957. (See photograph from author's collection taken in 1974. Another picture shows how alone the grave is, in comparison with other sections of the cemetery.)

In Silver's book (page 21) she writes, "The grave alone gives peace." This also now applies to Silver.

Poor Silver was a very unfortunate girl. She had experienced so many disappointments and failures in life. She gave up the struggle. Baby Doe was heart-broken. She had tried so hard to keep Silver from sin. She was always haunted by her visions of Silver. She said, "The devils are after my Silver." She continued to have visions of a tragic end for this child she loved so much. Baby Doe had sacrificed everything for Silver. A last vision Baby Doe had was that this deceased daughter rode up to the shack on a golden horse. This dream was recorded on her calendar. Was Silver a victim of circumstances? She was drawn into the slums of Chicago and had been too weak to resist the wicked ways of life.

I was impressed with Silver's touching account of the fate of Artie Dallas. It occurs to me that some of this same fate parallels Silver's own life. "No friend visits her lowly grave, but perhaps occasionally a wild bird hovers over the lonely spot, chanting a carol whose plaintive notes ascend into the infinite realms above and invocate, 'Be merciful to her, for she

**One of the last pictures of Silver Dollar. On the
lake front in Chicago, 1925.**

Grave of Silver Dollar (left foreground) in Holy Sepulchre Cemetery, Chicago. Note how "alone" the grave is.

ROSE MARY ECHO
SILVER DOLLAR TABOR
1889 ✟ 1925
REST IN PEACE

Headstone at grave of Silver Dollar. Photo taken in 1974.

Evelyn E. Furman Collection

Front entrance to the Holy Sepulchre Cemetery in Chicago, 1974.

knew not what she did.' She had fiducially answered the call of death and she faded, rapidly and silently as a flower.

"There in a notorious resort in the underworld, she closed her eyes, her wild, startled black eyes that hopelessly flashed from out her flying dark hair.

"It was all ended; Artie was gone. No more would she rove the streets bareheaded, with the winter wind pitilessly cutting her half-naked body, in a mad effort to find food and shelter; never again would she be found drunk in the market street gutters; never again would Artie suffer."

Many years have gone by, and I read this page again. It reminds me of poor Silver—her grave, her answer to the call of death, just as Silver died in the underworld of Chicago, It was all ended. Silver was gone; no more would she be seeking food and shelter. Never again would she be found drunk, never again would Silver suffer.

If only Silver had heeded the words she herself wrote (page 70), "Go back to the home where love and respect is your dower, for you will never find it here."

Silver used words from the Bible in her book (page 72)—"The sins of the father and mother shall be visited upon the children, even unto the fourth and fifth generations." She adds: "It has been historically so and will be eternally so."

And on page 73: "Therefore this child of kismet and atavism Allen Hence Dawnen, is more to be pitied than condemned, for he could not master the intangible power that controlled him."

Silver, also a child of a terrible fate, is "more to be pitied than condemned." Thus we come to the end of the story of Silver Dollar Tabor.

## Chapter Sixteen
# *Mistress of the Matchless Mine*

But the story of Baby Doe was not over. A newspaper article from the Leadville paper indicates that perhaps her luck was changing.

Leadville, Colorado, June 9

Winfield S. Stratton, millionaire mine owner of Cripple Creek, has redeemed the Matchless mine in Leadville for the widow of the late Senator Tabor. Years ago Senator Tabor advanced some money to Stratton when the latter was a poor struggling miner, and he never forgot it. When Tabor died he had lost almost everything, and he was mainly endeavoring to save the Matchless mine, which he always insisted still contained millions in its lower contracts, never explored. The property was sold some months ago at sheriff's sale, and final title would pass on July 4 to the new owners.

For a year past, Mrs. Tabor has been endeavoring to save the mine, but despite the fact that there are hundreds of persons in Colorado whom Tabor helped when he was rich, she could not raise the money. Mr. Stratton heard of her trouble, and assured her that if the title to the property was all right that he would assist her. The title is clear, and a check for $15,000 will be paid over tomorrow, and the title revert to Stratton who will on July 4 turn the mine over to Mrs. Tabor.

This is the day that Stratton discovered the Independence mine which made him famous, and it is a strange coincidence that on this day he now returns a kindness to the widow and family of the man who helped him when he was poor. Mr. Stratton will furnish the money to push the shaft to the lower contracts, where Senator Tabor always insisted there are as many millions hidden away as were taken out of the Matchless mine in

A drawing of Baby Doe, mistress of the Matchless Mine.

its palmiest days when over a million dollars was extracted in ninety days from the upper workings. This appears like a new start for the widow who has met with every misfortune since her husband's death and who has been compelled to take in washing at times to keep starvation from the door of herself and her children. Senator Tabor was one of the best known characters of the West. He spent his millions freely and died a poor man. It was he who gave the city of Denver its first start.

But Baby Doe was still troubled with more claims against the Matchless. In April 1927 the Shorego Mining Company, owned by the Mullen interests, foreclosed on the mortgage on the mine. They never evicted Baby Doe or attempted to work the mine. She continued to live at the Matchless, guarding the mine, alone with her memories. She often walked to Leadville, and stopped in to visit her friends. Baby Doe's friends visited her at the mine, but if a stranger knocked at her door, she never would answer.

She refused to accept charity. Her brother Peter McCourt passed away and another brother Willard still lived in Denver.

In July of 1930 Phillip McCourt, also from Denver, came up to help Baby Doe with the Matchless. They both set about getting the mine ready to work once more. It was not known just where the money came from for this venture. Workmen were employed cleaning up the place to make ready for action. They moved in an old boiler at No. 6 shaft, and prepared to sink the shaft to a further depth. At the end of each day, the workmen were paid regularly. Finally the pay stopped, and work stopped. Again it was the same story. Capital ran out before they reached pay dirt. Another dream faded away, and where was the Tabor luck of the past?

In 1933 the author moved to Leadville, and had employment there for the summer. My intentions were to return to college, back in Wisconsin, that fall. I had seen Baby Doe and soon heard the Tabor story which fascinated me. I married a miner, and we lived up the mountain above the Matchless. We lived at the cabin on the Silver Spoon mine in order to be near my husband's work. Driving to Leadville for groceries and supplies, we sometimes saw Baby Doe walking on Leadville streets. Usually she would be walking up Seventh Street headed for her cabin. She was a familiar character in Leadville. Dressed in her old garb she always looked the same. She wore a dark colored coat and a motoring cap, popular in the early twenties.

She sometimes had a long, flimsy scarf tied over the cap. Wherever she went, she always carried a large cloth-like bag. My father-in-law walked past the Matchless daily on his way to work in Leadville. After he had read his Denver newspaper he saved it and gave it to Baby Doe the next day. If he didn't see her around, he would leave the paper for her anyway. She loved to keep up with the news. She often spent hours reading in the library. Ellen, a good-hearted librarian in Leadville, gave her magazines. The years passed by and Baby Doe's life pattern remained about the same as always. On March 7, 1935 Baby Doe was found dead in her shack at the Matchless. She died alone, and the real cause of her death was not known. Coroner James Corbett gave the cause of her death as possibly a heart attack, and she is thought to have died February 20th. It is very likely that she caught cold on her last trip to Leadville. She was her own doctor, and all alone there with no help she may have had pneumonia. The snow was very deep in the winter, and often banked over the windows. Blizzards would last for several days at that high altitude. Walls and ceilings of her shack were lined with heavy paper to keep out the cold. The floors were of rough boards and poor protection in winter. Tom French, a miner, and Sue Bonney, a friend, lived nearby. Sue checked at times to see if all was well with Mrs. Tabor. One day they noticed that there was no smoke coming from the chimney of Baby Doe's shack. They had not seen her for a while and became worried. They decided to go up to the Matchless and shoveled their way through the deep drifts of snow. There was no response to their knocks on the door. Becoming alarmed, they entered her shack through a window. There, they found her frozen body. Baby Doe was dead!

Baby Doe left many scribbled notes and records made on her calendar—which also served her as a diary. March 6, she wrote: Went down to Leadville from Matchless—the snow so terrible, I had to go down on my hands and knees and creep

**Recent photo of the Matchless.**

**Baby Doe's handwriting on this envelope is evidence of her lonely existence at the Matchless Mine.**

**Road leading from the Matchless to Leadville. Baby Doe often walked this route.**

**Another view of the Matchless. Photo by the author.**

Interior of
Baby Doe Tabor's
Cabin after her Death
Matchless Mine-
Leadville. Colo.

470

Baby Doe's cabin after her death. Looters ransacked it, taking
many of the items.

**Another view of Baby Doe's cabin after vandals and souvenir hunters ransacked the contents. Later the cabin was restored.**

Baby Doe and Deck Wilmouth in front of the shack at the Matchless, 1933.

**Horace and Baby Doe Tabor's final resting place, Mount Olivet Cemetery, Denver.**

MRS H.A.W BABY DOE TABOR
LEADVILLE, COLO

One of the last photographs of Baby Doe by the door of her cabin at the Matchless.

from my cabin door to 7th Street. Mr. Zaitz driver (Zaitz delivery truck) drove me to our get off place and he helped pull me to the cabin. I kept falling deep down through the snow every minute. God bless him."

Many more of Baby Doe's visions were recorded on her calendar, and small scraps of paper. Often she made notations on the back of old envelopes.

Elmer Kutzleb, employee of Frank Zaitz Merchantile Co., was the last person to see Baby Doe. He was the delivery man who gave her a ride in the delivery truck from the store to the Matchless. He carried in her groceries, and helped her into the cabin. On her trip down to Leadville, she had fallen in the snow. Her clothes were wet, and she had gotten very cold. She was so thankful to have a ride on the return trip.

February 20 on her calendar Baby Doe made the last entry, "went to town." What happened between that date and the discovery of her death is unknown.

Baby Doe had kept the pledge she made to her dying husband. He whispered with his last breath, "Hang on to the Matchless, it will be pay millions again."

The Tabor fortune was gone forever. Only several dollar bills and a few coins remained in her purse at the time of her death.

The news of the tragic ending of this famous woman spread rapidly around the country. Newspaper headlines told of her death, and retold her life story.

Baby Doe's brother, Willard McCourt, arrived from Denver to take care of the arrangements. A funeral was held at the Church of Annunciation in Leadville. She lay peacefully in the silk-lined grey steel casket.

Burial was in Mount Olivet cemetery, Denver. H.A.W. Tabor's body was exhumed from Calvary cemetery and placed beside Baby Doe. No longer would Baby Doe worry about the Matchless. No longer would she be haunted by the memory of Silver's tragic ending.

Look back to Silver's book and read once more the passage on page 7: "Why had this tender mother been doomed to helplessly witness such a career as her son Allen's? Out of a proud home where the word harmony expressed every passion, desire and act he sprang like a ———— weed ———"

This parallels the suffering of Silver's mother. Baby Doe was always haunted by Silver's terrible years in Chicago. Now Baby Doe would suffer no more.

The author has in her files an old newspaper clipping of 1935, written after the death of Baby Doe. It reads: "Silver Dollar's book was found among the effects in a trunk stored in a Denver warehouse. A corner of the page had been turned back so that the book opened there naturally (see page 21). Near the bottom of the page a sentence had been ringed with blue pencil: 'The grave alone gives peace.' " Who marked the passage or when is not known. Yes, Silver Dollar and Baby Doe both were now at peace.

After the death of Baby Doe, newspapers of the day stated that her daughter Lily who was living in Wisconsin, "denied through the closed door of her modest apartment at a busy uptown intersection here that she was the daughter of Baby Doe Tabor."

She seemed reluctant to speak to interviewers and denied them admittance to her apartment.

She said, however, that she was the daughter of John Tabor, a brother of the famed H.A.W. Tabor, who had dug a fortune in silver from the Matchless. She added that she had left Colorado years ago and that it was a common mistake to identify her as the daughter of the "Silver Dollar" Tabors.

Neighbors said they knew little of the Last family, stating that they saw them infrequently and rarely exchanged words with them.

It is not known if the facts presented in this story are true or not.

After Baby Doe's death the 17 iron trunks in storage in Denver were opened. In them were found several bolts of exquisite cloth which had never been cut, a Tiffany silver tea service, dressing table accessories, pieces of china, and other mementoes.

Baby Doe also left gunny sacks and four treasure-filled trunks with the sisters at old St. Vincent's Hospital. After her death, Baby Doe's jewelry was found in storage there. Included in the jewelry was a diamond and sapphire ring and

Mr. Tabor's famous watch fob and chain. Baby Doe, wanting her treasures in a safe place, left them at the Hospital, as she knew they would be stolen if kept in her cabin. Also found was a miner's candle holder wrapped in a sheet of paper. Silver had written on a piece of paper, "The Candle holder Mama used at the Matchless Mine."

In Mount Olivet cemetery, Baby Doe Tabor and her husband, H.A.W. Tabor, lie side by side in graves marked by an imposing monument. C.E. Liesveld of the G. & L. Granite Co. was the donor of the large stone. The border depicts the Matchless mine near Leadville, the source of Tabor's great wealth; the U.S. Capitol, symbolizing his senatorship, and a sunset, symbolizing death.

The unveiling of the monument took place March 31, 1940. On this occasion Mrs. Clyde Robertson, nationally known writer, read her poem—"Mistress of the Matchless Mine."

### Mistress of the Matchless Mine

*A blinding spot burned on the snow*
*Where no spot was; an undertow,*
*Where no sea ran, tugged at her feet—*
*A tom-tom drummed at maddening beat*
*Into her ears though not a sound*
*Fretted the air or frozen ground.*

*Once, she turned with a last farewell*
*To the camp below: "The years will tell*
*Who were the great and who the small!*
*He was greater than you all.*
*The ore runs rich and the veins run wide*
*In the silver hills on the Great Divide:*
*Wide and rich as the ore veins run,*
*He left his trail in the Western sun."*

*The spot on the snow grew red as blood*
*And she seemed to wade through a freezing flood*
*She would reach the shack! She would bar the door*
*On the jeering world as she'd done before.*
*She clutched the coin in her withered hand*
*With fingers stiff as a steely band.*

When she was dead and they found her there,
They would find she still had gold to spare.

Burned in her brain were the words he said,
He, greater than all, now long since dead:
"Swear by the saints you always will
Stay with the lode on Fryer Hill.
Stick like the roots of an old jack pine;
Never give up the Matchless Mine."

It had come to mean, as the years grew old,
Something more than a hill of gold;
It was not a mountain, it was a man
Glorified in a granite span!
It was not a mine, but flesh and blood
Caught in the swirl of a golden flood!

Her fumbling fingers forced the latch
And coaxed a spark from a sodden match.
Cold as the icy clutch of doom,
The black damp filtered through the room.
But the red spot followed and burned the wall

Till the bare room blazed like a banquet hall;
And there, in the golden circle, shown
The glamorous scenes she once had known.
The tattered quilt, in her dark death sweat,
Became a satin coverlet.
She was again the courted queen
And he a man of kingly mien.

A wildcat wailed on Fryer Hill,
A woman sighed, then all was still.
The last coin of her golden store
Fell from her hand; across the floor
A pilfering pack rat slyly stole
And dragged it off to his robber hole.
Still the faithful fingers cling
To a rosary —— a knotted string ——
A knotted string where a prayer still lingers,
Clasped in the quiet, calloused fingers.

*A gutted candle, black in the socket,*
*A man's face, in a tarnished locket,*
*A lean rat, making ready to leap,*
*A woman, open-eyed, asleep ——*

*She who could write with a scholar's pen,*
*She who could speak with the best of men,*
*She who had shone like a jeweled plaque ——*
*Dead with her dreams in a mountain shack.*

*Holy Mother, grant her peace,*
*Grant an uncontested lease*
*Beyond the Great Divide's dark line*
*To the Mistress of the Matchless Mine.*

## THE END